The Science of LUCID DREAMING

A Comprehensive Guide to Lucid Dreaming explores the latest scientific research and techniques for inducing and controlling lucid dreams

by

CASEY WILLIAMS

This publication is designed to provide accurate and authoritative information in regard to the subject matter covered. It is sold with the understanding that neither the author nor the publisher is engaged in rendering legal, investment, accounting or other professional services. While the publisher and author have used their best efforts in preparing this book, they make no representations or warranties with respect to the accuracy or completeness of the contents of this book and specifically disclaim any implied warranties of merchantability or fitness for a particular purpose. No warranty may be created or extended by sales representatives or written sales materials. The advice and strategies contained herein may not be suitable for your situation. You should consult with a professional when appropriate. Neither the publisher nor the author shall be liable for any loss of profit or any other commercial damages, including but not limited to special, incidental, consequential, personal, or other damages.

ISBN: 978-1-961140-03-5

Contents

Introduction

Welcome to the extraordinary world of lucid dreaming, where your wildest fantasies can become vivid realities and your sleeping mind becomes a playground for endless possibilities. This book is your gateway to unlocking the hidden depths of your consciousness and harnessing the power of lucid dreaming to transform your life.

Within these pages, we will embark on an enlightening journey that will introduce you to the concept of lucid dreaming, delve into its fascinating history, and explore the latest scientific research that unravels the mysteries of this incredible phenomenon. But this book is not merely a compendium of theories and facts; it is a practical guide that will equip you with the knowledge and techniques to experience lucid dreams for yourself.

Part I: Understanding Lucid Dreaming lays the foundation by unraveling the nature of lucid dreams. We will begin with Chapter 1, where we will define lucid dreaming and discover its origins, tracing its roots back through the annals of time. You will learn how lucid dreams differ from regular dreams, and through captivating examples, you will come to understand the power and potential that lie within these extraordinary experiences.

Chapter 2, The Science of Lucid Dreaming, will take you on an enthralling journey into the realm of scientific research. You will explore the cutting-edge discoveries that shed light on the neurobiology of dreaming and unravel the intricate workings of the dreaming brain. By delving into the latest studies, we will uncover the profound implications that these findings have for lucid dreaming and the remarkable benefits that can be derived from it.

Dreams have long captivated the human imagination, and in Chapter 3, Dream Interpretation, we will explore the art of deciphering their enigmatic messages. Through a variety of techniques, you will gain insights into how to unravel the symbolism and meaning embedded within your dreams. Furthermore, we will unveil the profound ways in which lucid dreaming can enhance your ability to interpret and understand the deeper layers of your subconscious mind.

Part II: Techniques for Inducing and Controlling Lucid Dreams takes you into the realm of practicality, providing you with a repertoire of proven methods to induce and maintain lucidity in your dreams. In Chapter 4, Reality Testing, you will discover the power of questioning your reality and cultivating self-awareness. We will explore various reality testing techniques that can serve as potent triggers for lucidity, empowering you to become a conscious participant in your dreams.

Chapter 5 unveils the Wake-Initiated Lucid Dreaming (WILD) technique—a powerful approach that allows you to transition seamlessly from wakefulness to the dream state while maintaining awareness. We will guide you through the step-by-step process of practicing WILD, equipping you with the tools to embark on awe-inspiring journeys within your lucid dreams. However, it is crucial to understand the potential challenges and risks associated with this technique, and we will explore these with the utmost care and consideration.

In Chapter 6, we will introduce the Mnemonic-Induced Lucid Dreaming (MILD) technique, which focuses on programming your mind to recognize and initiate lucid dreams. With detailed instructions and practical exercises, you will learn how to harness the power of intention and memory to manifest lucidity in your dreams. We will also delve into the benefits and potential challenges of the MILD technique, allowing you to navigate this approach with confidence and efficacy.

Chapter 7 broadens your repertoire of techniques by providing an overview of other proven methods for inducing lucid dreams. From the Wake-Back-to-Bed (WBTB) technique to the Finger Induced Lucid Dreaming (FILD) technique, you will have a comprehensive understanding of the different options available to you. We will also guide you in selecting the technique that aligns best with your unique needs and preferences, ensuring that you embark on your lucid dreaming journey with a sense of purpose and direction.

Part III: The Power of Lucid Dreaming delves into the transformative potential of lucid dreaming, illustrating how it can be harnessed for creative expression, healing, self-discovery, and mindfulness. In Chapter 8, we explore the remarkable connection between lucid dreaming and creativity. You will discover how lucid dreams can serve as a wellspring of inspiration for artists, writers, musicians, and creators of all kinds. We will provide you with techniques to harness the creative potential of your lucid dreams and unlock a realm of limitless imagination.

Chapter 9 delves into the profound healing and self-discovery capabilities of lucid dreaming. Within the lucid dream state, you can navigate the depths of your subconscious mind, address emotional traumas, and gain profound insights into your innermost self. We will guide you in utilizing lucid dreams as a catalyst for personal growth, self-improvement, and holistic healing, empowering you to embark on a transformative journey of self-discovery.

In Chapter 10, we explore the intersection of lucid dreaming and mindfulness, an ancient practice that cultivates present-moment awareness. Through the integration of mindfulness techniques into your lucid dreams, you can deepen your self-awareness, enhance the quality of your lucid experiences, and tap into the profound wisdom that lies within. We will provide you with practical exercises and guidance on merging these two powerful practices, unlocking a new level of consciousness and insight.

This book is not meant to be a mere intellectual exercise; it is an invitation to embark on a life-changing adventure. As we conclude this preface, we invite you to step boldly into the realm of lucid dreaming. With the knowledge, techniques, and guidance provided within these pages, you possess the keys to unlocking the extraordinary potential of your dreaming mind. The time has come to awaken your slumbering consciousness and embark on a journey that will forever transform your perception of reality.

Are you ready to take the first step? Let the adventure begin.

Part I

Understanding Lucid Dreaming

CHAPTER 1

What are Lucid Dreams?

INTRODUCTION

Welcome to the extraordinary realm of lucid dreaming, a realm where the boundaries of reality blur and the realms of imagination come alive. Close your eyes and imagine a world where you have the power to consciously shape and navigate your dreams, where the impossible becomes possible, and where the depths of your subconscious mind become a playground for exploration. This chapter marks the beginning of a remarkable journey into the fascinating world of lucid dreaming, where we will unravel the mysteries of this unique phenomenon and unlock the hidden potential within our dreamscapes.

In the hazy landscape of sleep, our minds weave intricate tapestries of dreams. We find ourselves transported to otherworldly realms, interacting with strange characters, and experiencing a myriad of emotions. But what if we could become fully aware that we are dreaming while still immersed in the dream itself? What if we could take control, shape the dream to our desires, and explore the depths of our subconscious with conscious intent? These are the wonders of lucid dreaming, a state of consciousness that transcends the boundaries of ordinary dreams and allows us to step into a realm of infinite possibilities.

Throughout history, lucid dreaming has captivated the minds of philosophers, mystics, and dream enthusiasts alike. Ancient civilizations, such as the Egyptians and the Greeks, recognized the existence of lucid dreaming and attributed spiritual significance to these ethereal experiences. In Egyptian culture, dreams were considered portals to the divine realm, where gods and goddesses communicated with mortals. The Greek philosopher Aristotle pondered the nature of dreams and questioned the distinction between wakefulness and the dream state. The fascination with lucid dreaming is not a recent phenomenon; it is an age-old inquiry into the mysteries of the human mind.

The term "lucid dreaming" itself was coined by Dutch psychiatrist and writer Frederik van Eeden in the early 20th century. Van Eeden, a visionary explorer of the dream realm, embarked on a personal quest to document and understand his own lucid dreams. His pioneering work brought lucid dreaming to the forefront of scientific inquiry and inspired countless others to explore the hidden depths of their own dreams. Since then, researchers, psychologists, and dream enthusiasts alike have dedicated themselves to unraveling the mysteries of lucid dreaming, leading to a wealth of knowledge and techniques that continue to evolve.

But what exactly is a lucid dream? A lucid dream can be defined as a dream in which the dreamer becomes aware that they are dreaming while still immersed in the dream itself. Unlike regular dreams, where we often passively observe events unfolding, lucid dreaming grants us the power to actively engage and navigate within the dream world. This heightened awareness enables us to recognize the dream's illusory nature and, in some cases, exert control over its unfolding narrative.

Imagine soaring through the skies like a majestic eagle, exploring distant galaxies, or conversing with historical figures long past. In a lucid dream, these experiences are not mere figments of our imagination; they become vivid realities that we can explore, interact with, and learn from. Lucid dreaming offers a gateway to a realm where the laws of physics bend and the constraints of reality dissolve. It opens up a world of infinite possibilities, where the only limits are the boundaries of our own minds.

As we embark on this journey of discovery, we will delve into the science behind lucid dreaming, exploring the latest research and understanding of this remarkable phenomenon. We will learn about the neurobiology of dreaming and how it relates to the experience of lucidity. We will uncover the techniques and practices that can induce and enhance lucid dreaming, empowering us to take control of our dream experiences. We will explore the profound impact lucid dreaming can have on our creativity, self-discovery, and personal growth. And ultimately, we will awaken to the power that lies within us as we bridge the gap between dreams and reality.

So, fasten your seatbelt and prepare for an adventure like no other. Open your mind to the infinite possibilities that await within the realm of lucid dreaming. Get ready to embark on a journey of self-discovery, exploration, and transformation. The dream world awaits, and it is time to unlock its secrets. Welcome to the extraordinary world of lucid dreaming.

DEFINING LUCID DREAMS

To truly understand the depth and wonder of lucid dreaming, it is essential to delve into its intricate nature and explore its various dimensions. Lucid dreams have captivated the human imagination for centuries, offering a tantalizing glimpse into the vast potential of the mind and its ability to shape our experiences even within the realm of dreams.

At its core, a lucid dream can be defined as a dream in which the dreamer becomes aware that they are dreaming while still immersed in the dream itself. This heightened state of consciousness sets lucid dreaming apart from regular dreams, where the dreamer remains unaware of the dream's illusory nature. In a lucid dream, the individual realizes, with utmost clarity, that they are in a realm of their own creation, a world shaped by the boundless depths of their imagination.

The concept of lucid dreaming opens up a gateway to a realm where the laws of physics bend and the constraints of reality dissolve. It is a space where the ordinary rules of the waking world cease to apply, and the only limitations are those imposed by our own beliefs and expectations. In this extraordinary state of awareness, we are free to explore, create, and interact with the dream environment in ways that defy the confines of the physical world.

Lucid dreams exist on a spectrum, ranging from partial lucidity to full lucidity. Partial lucidity refers to a state where the dreamer experiences moments of awareness within the dream but may not have complete control or continuity of lucidity. These moments of clarity may come and go, fleeting as they intertwine with the fluid nature of the dream narrative. Full lucidity, on the other hand, represents the pinnacle of lucid dreaming, where the dreamer possesses a profound sense of self-awareness and complete control over the dream's unfolding narrative. In this state, the dreamer becomes the master of their dreamscape, able to shape the environment, summon characters, and dictate the course of events with intention and purpose.

One of the distinguishing features of lucid dreams is the ability to perform reality checks within the dream state. These reality checks serve as a litmus test to determine whether one is in the waking world or within the realm of a dream. By developing the habit of reality testing in our waking lives, we are more likely to carry this practice into our dreams. In a lucid dream, reality checks can reveal the dream's illusory nature, triggering the realization that we are in fact dreaming. Common reality checks include looking at one's hands, trying to push a finger through the palm of the opposite hand, or questioning the consistency of the dream environment.

What sets lucid dreams apart is the profound sense of freedom and agency they offer. Once lucidity is established, the dreamer can actively engage with the dream world, exploring its depths and pushing the boundaries of what is possible. This active participation sets lucid dreams apart from regular dreams, where we often find ourselves as passive spectators to the dream's unfolding events. In lucid dreams, we can choose to soar through the skies, traverse the depths of the ocean, or visit far-flung places that defy the limitations of time and space. We can engage in conversations with dream characters, seek wisdom from our subconscious, and tap into our innermost desires and fears.

The power of lucid dreaming lies not only in the ability to shape the dream environment but also in the opportunity for self-reflection and personal growth. Lucid dreams serve as a canvas for self-exploration, allowing us to confront our fears, overcome challenges, and gain insights into our subconscious mind. The dream world becomes a stage where we can experiment with new ideas, test our limits, and gain a deeper understanding of ourselves.

Lucid dreaming is not solely confined to solitary exploration. Shared lucid dreaming, also known as mutual dreaming, is a phenomenon where two or more individuals experience a lucid dream together. In these shared dreamscapes, dreamers can interact, communicate, and even collaborate on shared goals or experiences. Shared lucid dreaming opens up possibilities for connection, collaboration, and the exploration of the dream realm as a shared consciousness.

As we journey further into the realm of lucid dreaming, we will explore the techniques, practices, and scientific understanding that underpin this remarkable phenomenon. We will delve into the neurobiology of dreaming, uncovering the brain processes that contribute to lucidity. We will unravel the various methods for inducing and enhancing lucid dreams, from reality testing to specialized techniques such as wake-initiated lucid dreaming (WILD) and mnemonic-induced lucid dreaming (MILD). We will also explore the potential benefits and risks associated with lucid dreaming, from enhancing creativity and problem-solving skills to managing nightmares and trauma.

In the pages that follow, prepare to be immersed in the multifaceted world of lucid dreaming. Let go of preconceived notions, open your mind to the extraordinary, and embrace the limitless possibilities that await within the realm of lucid dreams. Together, we will awaken to the power that lies within us as we bridge the gap between dreams and reality and embark on a journey of self-discovery, exploration, and transformation. The adventure begins now.

A JOURNEY THROUGH HISTORY

To fully appreciate the concept of lucid dreaming, we must embark on a journey through time, exploring its rich history and the fascination it has sparked in various cultures and civilizations. Lucid dreaming is not a recent discovery; it has captured the human imagination for centuries, weaving its way through folklore, philosophy, and spiritual practices.

Ancient civilizations were well acquainted with the phenomenon of lucid dreaming, albeit under different names and interpretations. In the ancient Egyptian civilization, dreams held great significance and were considered portals to the divine realm. Dreams were believed to be messages from the gods and to contain hidden meanings and prophecies. In Egyptian hieroglyphs, the word for dream, "rswt," was depicted as a person sleeping with their eyes wide open, suggesting an awareness within the dream state. The ability to be conscious in dreams was regarded as a sign of divine communication.

Similarly, in ancient Greek culture, dreams were considered a conduit between the mortal and divine realms. Philosopher Aristotle, in his work "On Dreams," contemplated the nature of dreams and questioned the distinction between the waking world and the dream state. He recognized that dreams could sometimes possess a sense of vividness and realism, blurring the boundaries between reality and imagination.

The concept of lucid dreaming found its way into Buddhist and Hindu teachings as well. In the Buddhist tradition, the practice of dream yoga involves training the mind to maintain awareness within dreams as a means of achieving enlightenment. The Indian sage Patanjali, in his Yoga Sutras, described the state of "svapna nidra," or lucid dreaming, where the dreamer possesses self-awareness and control over the dream narrative. These ancient practices reveal a profound understanding of the potential of the dream state as a vehicle for spiritual growth and self-realization.

The term "lucid dreaming," as we know it today, was coined by Dutch psychiatrist and writer Frederik van Eeden in the early 20th century. Van Eeden, an avid dream researcher, sought to document and understand his own experiences of conscious awareness within dreams. He published a series of articles and essays in which he detailed his personal explorations and observations of lucid dreaming. Van Eeden's groundbreaking work brought the phenomenon of lucid dreaming to the attention of the scientific community and paved the way for further research and exploration.

In the mid-20th century, the field of dream research experienced a significant expansion with the pioneering work of psychologist Celia Green. Her book "Lucid Dreams" delved into the psychological and philosophical implications of lucid dreaming, examining its potential as a tool for self-discovery and personal growth. Green's work served as a catalyst for the scientific investigation of lucid dreaming, igniting interest and sparking further research.

Since then, numerous researchers, psychologists, and dream enthusiasts have dedicated themselves to unraveling the mysteries of lucid dreaming. Scientific studies have explored the neurobiology of dreaming, shedding light on the brain processes that contribute to the experience of lucidity. Advances in technology, such as electroencephalography (EEG) and functional magnetic resonance imaging (fMRI), have allowed researchers to peer into the sleeping brain and gain insights into the mechanisms underlying lucid dreaming.

With the advent of the internet, the sharing of personal experiences and lucid dreaming techniques has become more accessible than ever before. Online communities and forums have blossomed, providing a platform for dreamers from all walks of life to exchange insights, techniques, and anecdotes. Lucid dreaming has transitioned from a niche topic within scientific circles to a subject of popular interest, capturing the curiosity of individuals seeking to explore the untapped potential of their own dreams.

As we continue our journey through the pages of this book, we will uncover the techniques and practices that have been developed over time to induce and enhance lucid dreaming. We will also explore the scientific research that has deepened our understanding of this extraordinary phenomenon. By building upon the wisdom and discoveries of those who came before us, we can embark on our own personal exploration of the realm of lucid dreaming.

Through this historical exploration, we come to realize that lucid dreaming is not merely a passing fascination but a timeless and universal human experience. Across cultures and throughout history, the pursuit of conscious awareness within dreams has captivated the minds of philosophers, mystics, and scholars alike. It is a testament to the enduring allure of the dream world and the profound potential it holds for self-discovery and transformation.

As we step forward into the realm of lucid dreaming, let us honor the wisdom of those who paved the way and embark on our own quest to unlock the hidden depths of the dream world. The journey continues, and the wonders of lucid dreaming await us.

DISTINGUISHING LUCID DREAMS FROM REGULAR DREAMS

To truly grasp the essence of lucid dreaming, it is vital to explore how it differs from regular dreams. While regular dreams often unfold with a sense of passivity, where we are carried along by the currents of our subconscious mind, lucid dreams offer a remarkable departure from this norm. Within the realm of lucidity, we find ourselves endowed with a profound sense of self-awareness, actively participating in and influencing the dream narrative.

One of the fundamental distinctions between lucid dreams and regular dreams lies in the level of consciousness we possess during the dream state. In a regular dream, our awareness is typically limited, and we accept the dream events and surroundings as real without questioning their authenticity. We become immersed in the dream narrative, often unaware of the dream's illusory nature. In contrast, lucid dreams are characterized by a heightened state of consciousness where we recognize, with utmost clarity, that we are dreaming while still immersed in the dream itself. This realization sets the stage for a transformative experience in the dream world.

Lucidity within dreams can manifest in different degrees, ranging from partial awareness to full lucidity. In partial lucidity, we experience fleeting moments of awareness within the dream, where we may question the events or circumstances briefly before returning to the flow of the dream narrative. These fleeting moments of clarity serve as glimpses into the potential of lucid dreaming, teasing us with the possibility of deeper exploration and self-awareness. Full lucidity, however, represents the pinnacle of the lucid dreaming experience, where we possess a profound sense of self-awareness, complete control over our actions, and the ability to shape the dream environment at will.

Another distinguishing factor between lucid dreams and regular dreams lies in the degree of control we have over the dream narrative. In regular dreams, we often find ourselves as passive spectators, swept along by the whims of our subconscious mind. The dream events and characters unfold beyond our control, with a sense of detachment from our waking selves. In lucid dreams, however, we transcend this passive role and become active participants in the dream world. We can manipulate the dream environment, summon objects or characters, and alter the course of events with intention and purpose. The dream world becomes a canvas for our imagination, a realm where the boundaries of what is possible are expanded.

One of the distinguishing features of lucid dreaming is the ability to perform reality checks within the dream state. Reality checks serve as a tool to differentiate between the waking world and the dream world, enabling us to become aware of the dream's illusory nature. By incorporating reality testing into our waking lives, such as regularly questioning our reality or performing specific actions like trying to push a finger through the palm of our hand, we develop a habit that can carry over into our dreams. In a lucid dream, performing a reality check can trigger the realization that we are indeed dreaming, catapulting us into a state of lucidity.

Furthermore, the experience of sensory perception in lucid dreams can be remarkably vivid and immersive. The dream environment can be as vivid and lifelike as the waking world, engaging all our senses with heightened intensity. Colors may appear more vibrant, textures more palpable, and sounds more vivid. This heightened sensory experience contributes to the sense of realism within lucid dreams and further distinguishes them from regular dreams, where sensory perception can be more subdued or distorted.

The passage of time within lucid dreams can also differ from that in regular dreams. In regular dreams, the perception of time can be fluid and distorted, with events and sequences unfolding in a nonlinear fashion. In contrast, lucid dreams can provide a heightened awareness of time, allowing us to gauge the duration of the dream and engage with a sense of continuity. This temporal coherence within lucid dreams contributes to a more structured and intentional experience, fostering a deeper engagement with the dream narrative.

It is worth noting that while lucid dreaming offers extraordinary possibilities for self-exploration and personal growth, regular dreams hold their own significance and value. Regular dreams can serve as a window into our subconscious mind, revealing hidden emotions, desires, and unresolved conflicts. They provide a space for processing our daily experiences, allowing the mind to weave narratives and make sense of the complexities of life. Regular dreams can inspire creativity, offer solace, or even present us with symbolic messages that hold profound meaning for our waking lives.

In conclusion, lucid dreams stand apart from regular dreams by offering a heightened state of consciousness, a sense of self-awareness, and the ability to actively participate in and shape the dream narrative. Through lucidity, we transcend the passive role of an observer and become active agents within the dream world. By understanding the distinctions between lucid dreams and regular dreams, we can appreciate the unique qualities and transformative potential that lucid dreaming holds. The stage is set, and as we delve deeper into this fascinating realm, we shall uncover the techniques and practices that allow us to navigate the landscape of lucidity with confidence and awe.

THE SPECTRUM OF LUCIDITY

Within the realm of lucid dreaming, there exists a wide spectrum of experiences, ranging from fleeting moments of awareness to profound and immersive states of lucidity. Understanding the nuances of this spectrum is crucial for comprehending the diverse range of experiences that lucid dreaming offers.

At one end of the spectrum, we find those subtle instances of lucidity where a glimmer of awareness arises within the dream. These brief moments can be likened to a flickering candle in the darkness, illuminating the dreamer's consciousness before fading back into the depths of the dream narrative. Such instances may manifest as a passing thought or a sense of questioning the dream's authenticity, only to be swiftly engulfed by the dream's unfolding events. These subtle hints of lucidity can serve as an introduction to the possibilities of conscious dreaming, sparking curiosity and igniting the desire for further exploration.

Moving along the spectrum, we encounter a state of partial lucidity. In these experiences, the dreamer possesses a higher level of awareness and cognition within the dream but may not fully grasp the dream's illusory nature. Partial lucidity often involves moments of critical reflection or questioning, where the dreamer pauses to evaluate the dream events or attempts to exert some influence over the narrative. Although these glimpses of lucidity may be brief and sporadic, they offer tantalizing glimpses into the potential for greater self-awareness and dream control.

Continuing along the spectrum, we arrive at a state of moderate lucidity. Here, the dreamer attains a more consistent and substantial level of awareness within the dream. They become increasingly conscious of their dream state and may actively engage with the dream narrative, making deliberate choices and exerting influence over the dream environment. In this state, the dreamer may possess a sense of agency, shaping the dream's unfolding events and exploring the dream landscape with intention and purpose. The dreamer may experiment with various actions, such as flying, changing the dream scenery, or engaging in conversations with dream characters. Moderate lucidity provides a taste of the transformative potential of lucid dreaming, allowing the dreamer to actively participate in their own dream experiences.

As we progress further along the spectrum, we encounter the realm of full lucidity. This represents the pinnacle of the lucid dreaming experience, where the dreamer possesses a profound and unwavering awareness of their dream state. In a fully lucid dream, the dreamer is acutely conscious of the fact that they are dreaming, with a deep understanding that the dream environment is a creation of their own mind. This heightened state of self-awareness empowers the dreamer to exert an extraordinary degree of control over the dream narrative, manipulating the dream environment and characters with ease. Within full lucidity, the dreamer can explore limitless possibilities, engage in profound self-reflection, and embark on transformative journeys within the dream realm.

Beyond full lucidity, some dreamers report experiences that transcend traditional boundaries and push the limits of what we understand about lucid dreaming. These experiences, often referred to as "lucid dream superpowers" or "advanced lucid dreaming," involve extraordinary abilities within the dream state. Examples of these abilities include advanced telekinesis, time manipulation, heightened sensory perception, and even communication with higher-dimensional beings. While these experiences may lie at the far end of the spectrum and may be less common, they serve as a testament to the expansiveness and boundless potential of the lucid dreaming experience.

It is important to note that the spectrum of lucidity is not fixed or rigid. Each individual may traverse different points along the spectrum, and the level of lucidity experienced can vary from dream to dream. Factors such as practice, intention, and personal circumstances can influence where one falls on the spectrum during any given lucid dreaming experience.

By understanding the spectrum of lucidity, we gain a broader perspective on the possibilities and potential of lucid dreaming. Whether we find ourselves in the subtle hints of awareness, the moderate engagement with the dream narrative, or the profound realms of full lucidity, each point along the spectrum offers unique opportunities for self-exploration, personal growth, and awe-inspiring adventures within the world of dreams.

THE FASCINATION AND INTRIGUE OF LUCID DREAMING

Lucid dreaming has captivated the human imagination for centuries, evoking a sense of fascination and intrigue that transcends cultural and historical boundaries. The very notion of being able to consciously explore and interact with the dream world has ignited curiosity, sparked philosophical debates, and fueled artistic endeavors. This fascination with lucid dreaming stems from its ability to bridge the realms of the conscious and unconscious, offering a unique window into the depths of the human psyche.

One of the primary reasons for the fascination surrounding lucid dreaming is its inherent mystery. The dream world has long been recognized as a realm of symbolic and enigmatic experiences, where the boundaries of reality are blurred and the subconscious mind takes center stage. Lucid dreaming, with its potential for self-awareness and control within this mysterious realm, represents a doorway to unraveling the secrets of our own inner world. It offers a chance to explore the hidden recesses of the mind, confront unresolved emotions, and gain insights into our deepest desires and fears.

The allure of lucid dreaming also lies in its transformative potential. As we navigate the dream world with lucidity, we gain the opportunity to break free from the constraints of our everyday lives and explore uncharted territories. We can unleash our creativity, test the limits of our imagination, and engage in experiences that may be impossible or impractical in waking life. Lucid dreaming serves as a playground for personal growth, offering a safe space to confront challenges, overcome fears, and develop new skills. Through lucidity, we can actively participate in our own self-discovery and cultivate a deeper understanding of ourselves.

The notion of lucid dreaming as a gateway to extraordinary experiences has further fueled its fascination. Within the lucid dream state, we can embark on adventures that defy the laws of physics, travel to fantastical landscapes, or engage in encounters with mythical beings. We can fly through the skies, explore ancient civilizations, or engage in conversations with historical figures. Lucid dreaming opens up a realm of limitless possibilities where the boundaries of what is deemed possible in waking life are shattered. This potential for extraordinary experiences enthralls us and compels us to dive deeper into the practice of lucid dreaming.

Moreover, the scientific exploration of lucid dreaming has added a layer of intrigue to its study. Advances in neuroscience and psychology have shed light on the underlying mechanisms and brain activity associated with lucid dreaming. Research has revealed the neural correlates of lucidity, highlighting the areas of the brain responsible for self-awareness and metacognition. The scientific investigation of lucid dreaming not only enhances our understanding of this phenomenon but also underscores its significance as a unique state of consciousness worthy of exploration.

In addition to the personal and scientific fascination, the cultural impact of lucid dreaming cannot be overlooked. Throughout history, various cultures have held beliefs and practices related to lucid dreaming. In ancient civilizations, such as the Egyptians and the Greeks, dreams were seen as portals to divine messages and prophetic visions. Indigenous cultures, like the Aboriginal tribes of Australia or the Native American tribes, have incorporated lucid dreaming into their spiritual practices, using it as a means of connecting with the spiritual realm or gaining wisdom from ancestors. The rich tapestry of cultural perspectives on lucid dreaming adds depth and diversity to its allure, reminding us of its enduring significance across time and geography.

As we delve deeper into the realms of lucid dreaming, it is this fascination and intrigue that serve as our guide. The mysteries, possibilities, and transformative potential of lucid dreaming beckon us to explore, experiment, and uncover the hidden depths of our own consciousness. With each lucid dream, we inch closer to unraveling the enigma of the dream world and discovering the true extent of our own potential.

CONCLUSION

In conclusion, Chapter 1 has provided us with a comprehensive introduction to the fascinating world of lucid dreaming. We have embarked on a journey of exploration, delving into the depths of what lucid dreaming is, how it differs from regular dreams, and the spectrum of experiences it offers. Throughout this chapter, we have witnessed the captivating allure and intrigue that surround lucid dreaming, as well as its transformative potential and cultural significance.

We began our exploration by defining lucid dreams as those in which the dreamer becomes aware that they are dreaming while still within the dream. This heightened state of consciousness sets lucid dreams apart from regular dreams, allowing individuals to actively engage and shape the dream narrative. We discussed the various ways in which lucid dreams can be distinguished from regular dreams, including the presence of self-awareness, the ability to exercise control, and the potential for vivid and immersive experiences.

A journey through history took us on a captivating tour of how lucid dreaming has been understood and valued across different cultures and time periods. From ancient civilizations to contemporary scientific research, lucid dreaming has intrigued and fascinated humanity. We explored how lucid dreaming was seen as a gateway to the divine, a source of prophetic visions, and a means of connecting with the spiritual realm. We witnessed its integration into various cultural practices, highlighting its enduring significance and universal appeal.

The spectrum of lucidity presented us with a deeper understanding of the range of experiences that lucid dreaming encompasses. From subtle hints of awareness to profound states of full lucidity, each point along the spectrum offers unique opportunities for self-exploration, personal growth, and engagement with the dream world. We recognized that lucid dreaming is not a fixed state but rather a dynamic and fluid experience that can vary from dream to dream and from individual to individual.

The fascination and intrigue surrounding lucid dreaming have been the driving forces behind its exploration and study. We explored how lucid dreaming captivates our imagination, entices us with its transformative potential, and offers a gateway to extraordinary experiences. The allure of lucid dreaming lies in its ability to bridge the realms of the conscious and unconscious, providing a unique window into the depths of the human psyche. We also acknowledged the scientific investigation of lucid dreaming, which has shed light on its neural correlates and further enhanced our understanding of this extraordinary state of consciousness.

As we conclude this chapter, we stand on the threshold of a remarkable journey. We have laid the foundation for understanding lucid dreaming, exploring its history, distinguishing it from regular dreams, and appreciating its allure. The stage is set for us to delve deeper into the techniques, practices, and applications of lucid dreaming in the chapters to come.

Let us embark on this adventure with curiosity, open minds, and a willingness to explore the hidden realms of our own consciousness. Lucid dreaming awaits us, offering boundless possibilities for self-discovery, personal growth, and extraordinary experiences. Together, let us embrace the power of lucid dreaming and embark on a transformative journey that will forever expand our understanding of the human mind and the vast potential it holds within the realm of dreams.

CHAPTER 2

The Science of Lucid Dreaming

INTRODUCTION

Welcome to Chapter 2. Within the pages of this chapter, we invite you to embark on an awe-inspiring journey deep into the enthralling realm of the science behind lucid dreaming. Here, we will unravel the mysteries of the brain and its intricate activities during these extraordinary dreams. Prepare to be astounded as we delve into the wondrous world of neurobiology and uncover the secrets that lie within the enigmatic realm of lucid dreaming.

Lucid dreaming, with its inherent ability to grant conscious awareness and control within the realm of dreams, has captured human fascination for centuries. It is a phenomenon that has piqued the curiosity of scholars, philosophers, and dreamers alike, spurring countless investigations into its nature, origins, and potential applications. While lucid dreaming has been explored from various perspectives, it is through the lens of scientific research that we aim to bring forth a deeper understanding of this phenomenon.

The study of the neurobiology of dreaming, particularly lucid dreaming, has experienced significant advancements in recent years. With the advent of sophisticated brain imaging techniques and neuroscientific methodologies, researchers have been able to peer into the intricate workings of the brain during the dream state. Through their meticulous investigations, they have unraveled remarkable insights into the neural mechanisms that underlie the experience of lucidity within dreams.

The neurobiology of dreaming extends beyond the realm of lucid dreaming alone, encompassing the broader landscape of dream research. It entails a multifaceted exploration of brain activities, cognitive processes, and neurotransmitter systems that orchestrate the symphony of dreams. Within this vast expanse of inquiry, lucid dreaming shines as a beacon, beckoning us to unravel the intricate dance of consciousness and self-awareness within the dreaming mind.

As we journey deeper into the science behind lucid dreaming, we will encounter a tapestry of captivating discoveries. We shall navigate through the neural pathways that ignite the vivid tapestry of dreams and explore the regions of the brain that orchestrate the delicate balance between illusion and reality. It is within the framework of neurobiology that we shall uncover the threads that connect consciousness, cognition, and the enigmatic nature of dreams.

Through the utilization of cutting-edge neuroimaging technologies such as functional magnetic resonance imaging (fMRI) and electroencephalography (EEG), scientists have been able to peer into the depths of the dreaming brain. These tools allow us to observe and decipher the intricate symphony of neural activities that manifest during the wondrous experience of lucid dreaming. Such advancements have paved the way for a deeper understanding of the underlying mechanisms that grant us conscious control within the realm of dreams.

Moreover, the quest to comprehend the neurobiology of lucid dreaming has led researchers to investigate the intricate interplay of neurotransmitters within the dreaming brain. Among them, dopamine, a neurotransmitter renowned for its role in reward and pleasure systems, has emerged as a key player in the experience of lucidity. Scientists have explored the fluctuation of dopamine levels during the sleep-wake cycle, uncovering intriguing associations between dopamine and the occurrence of vivid dreams, including lucid dreams.

Intriguingly, the cognitive and psychological implications of lucid dreaming extend far beyond the realm of neuroscience. The exploration of lucid dreaming as a tool for personal growth, creative expression, and therapeutic applications has opened up a vast landscape of possibilities. Researchers and dream enthusiasts alike have tapped into the potential of lucid dreaming to foster self-discovery, enhance problem-solving abilities, and facilitate emotional healing.

In this chapter, we shall traverse the landscapes of neurobiology, psychology, and the human experience, unraveling the intricate tapestry that weaves together the science behind lucid dreaming. Together, we shall journey into the depths of the dreaming mind, guided by the illuminating torchlight of scientific inquiry.

So, dear reader, prepare to be immersed in the riveting world of lucid dreaming's neurobiological underpinnings. Brace yourself for a captivating exploration of the brain's enigmatic activities during lucid dreams. As we venture further, the secrets of the dreaming mind shall be unveiled, offering profound insights into the nature of consciousness, the depths of human potential, and the extraordinary possibilities that await within the realm of lucid dreaming.

THE NEUROBIOLOGY OF DREAMING

To truly grasp the science behind lucid dreaming, we must embark on a comprehensive exploration of the neurobiology of dreaming itself. Dreaming, a phenomenon that has intrigued and mystified humanity for centuries, is now being unraveled through the lens of neuroscience. As we delve into the intricacies of the brain's activities during dreaming, we shall uncover the fascinating interplay of neural networks, neurotransmitters, and brain regions that contribute to the rich tapestry of dream experiences.

One of the fundamental aspects of dreaming is its association with different stages of sleep. Within the sleep cycle, dreams predominantly occur during the rapid eye movement (REM) stage, characterized by heightened brain activity and vivid mental imagery. It is at this stage that lucid dreams often emerge, offering a unique platform for conscious exploration of the dream world.

Intriguingly, research has revealed that the brain engages in distinct patterns of activity during REM sleep. The visual cortex, responsible for processing visual information, becomes highly active during dreams, explaining the vivid and immersive nature of dream experiences. Other brain regions, such as the hippocampus involved in memory consolidation, the amygdala associated with emotional processing, and the prefrontal cortex responsible for higher-order cognitive functions, also exhibit intricate interactions during dreaming.

The prefrontal cortex, in particular, has garnered significant attention in the study of lucid dreaming. This region of the brain, involved in self-awareness, decision-making, and introspection, plays a crucial role in maintaining consciousness and control during lucid dreams. Studies using neuroimaging techniques, such as fMRI, have shown increased activity in the prefrontal cortex during lucid dreaming, suggesting its importance in the experience of lucidity and the ability to exert deliberate influence over dream narratives.

Furthermore, the brain's ability to generate and synchronize electrical activity in specific frequency ranges is also essential for dream experiences. Brainwave oscillations, such as gamma, alpha, theta, and delta waves, have been linked to different cognitive states and play a significant role in the manifestation of dreams. During lucid dreaming, gamma frequency oscillations, associated with conscious awareness and focused attention, appear to be heightened, contributing to the experience of heightened self-awareness within dreams.

Neurotransmitters, the chemical messengers of the brain, also play a crucial role in dreaming. Acetylcholine, in particular, has been implicated in the generation of REM sleep and the occurrence of vivid dreams. Studies have shown that acetylcholine levels are elevated during REM sleep, correlating with the presence of intense dream experiences. It is believed that this neurotransmitter facilitates the activation of visual and emotional brain regions, contributing to the immersive nature of dreams.

Additionally, the role of dopamine, a neurotransmitter associated with reward and motivation, has been investigated in the context of lucid dreaming. Research suggests that dopamine levels fluctuate during the sleep-wake cycle and are particularly elevated during REM sleep. This finding raises intriguing questions about the potential involvement of dopamine in the occurrence of lucid dreams. Genetic variations related to dopamine receptors have also been identified as potential contributors to individual differences in the propensity for lucid dreaming.

The intricate interplay of neurotransmitters, neural networks, and brain regions during dreaming highlights the complexity of the dreaming mind. It underscores the remarkable capabilities of the brain to create immersive worlds within the realm of dreams and hints at the untapped potential for conscious exploration and self-discovery within lucid dreams.

Furthermore, advancements in technology have allowed researchers to delve deeper into the neurobiology of dreaming. Techniques such as transcranial magnetic stimulation (TMS) and neurofeedback have been explored as tools to induce lucid dreams and modulate brain activity during dreaming. These experimental approaches offer exciting prospects for further unraveling the neural mechanisms underlying lucid dreaming and opening doors to new possibilities for therapeutic interventions and personal growth.

In conclusion, the neurobiology of dreaming provides a captivating framework for understanding the science behind lucid dreaming. The interplay of neural networks, neurotransmitters, and brain regions during REM sleep illuminates the intricate tapestry that gives rise to dream experiences. By delving into the depths of the dreaming mind, we gain profound insights into the mechanisms that allow for conscious awareness and control within the realm of dreams. As we continue our exploration, we will unravel additional layers of the scientific puzzle and discover the remarkable potential that lucid dreaming holds for personal growth, creativity, and self-discovery.

THE DISCOVERY OF LUCID DREAMING

The exploration of lucid dreaming dates back centuries, with accounts and anecdotes of individuals experiencing conscious awareness within their dreams. However, it was not until the modern era that lucid dreaming began to receive scientific attention and recognition. In this section, we will journey through the historical milestones that have shaped our understanding of lucid dreaming, from its early mentions in ancient cultures to its emergence as a subject of scientific inquiry.

1. Ancient Origins and Early References:

The roots of lucid dreaming can be traced back to ancient civilizations, where dreams held significant cultural and spiritual importance. In the writings of ancient civilizations such as the Greeks, Egyptians, and Indigenous cultures, we find references to dream experiences that bear striking resemblances to what we now call lucid dreaming. These accounts depict individuals who were aware they were dreaming and could actively engage with the dream world.

One of the earliest recorded mentions of lucid dreaming can be found in the writings of the Greek philosopher Aristotle, who contemplated the nature of dreams and the potential for conscious awareness within them. Plato, another Greek philosopher, also touched upon the subject, suggesting that dreams could be a reflection of the soul's desires and that one could exercise control over their dream experiences.

In the East, ancient Buddhist and Hindu texts, such as the Yoga Vasistha and the Upanishads, contain references to the concept of "dream yoga" or "yoga of the dream state." These texts describe practices aimed at achieving lucidity within dreams as a means of spiritual awakening and self-realization.

Throughout history, individuals from different cultures and eras have reported lucid dream experiences, often associating them with supernatural abilities or spiritual phenomena. However, it was not until the 19th century that lucid dreaming caught the attention of Western scholars and researchers.

2. Scientific Inquiry and Exploration:

The birth of scientific interest in lucid dreaming can be attributed to the influential work of French physician and neurologist Alfred Maury. In the mid-19th century, Maury published a groundbreaking book titled "Le Sommeil et les Reves" ("Sleep and Dreams"), in which he recounted his own experiences of lucid dreaming and explored the potential for conscious awareness within dreams.

Maury's work sparked the curiosity of subsequent researchers, including the pioneering psychologist and philosopher Frederik van Eeden. Van Eeden, in the early 20th century, coined the term "lucid dreaming" and began conducting systematic observations and experiments to investigate the phenomenon. He documented his own lucid dream experiences and collected reports from other individuals who claimed to have had similar experiences.

The interest in lucid dreaming continued to grow throughout the 20th century, with notable contributions from psychologists such as Celia Green, who published the influential book "Lucid Dreams" in 1968. Green's work not only provided a comprehensive exploration of lucid dreaming but also raised important questions about the nature of consciousness and the boundaries between dreaming and waking reality.

In the 1970s, advancements in sleep research and the development of electroencephalography (EEG) enabled scientists to investigate the physiological correlates of lucid dreaming. Pioneering studies by researchers like Stephen LaBerge at Stanford University demonstrated that lucid dreaming was a verifiable and distinct state of consciousness that could be identified and studied in the laboratory.

LaBerge's work also introduced innovative techniques for inducing lucid dreams, such as the use of reality testing and the development of the "Mnemonic Induction of Lucid Dreams" (MILD) technique. These approaches, based on the principles of awareness and intention, provided practical methods for individuals to increase their likelihood of experiencing lucid dreams.

3. Advancements in Neuroscience and Technology:

The turn of the 21st century witnessed a surge in scientific interest in lucid dreaming, driven by advancements in neuroscience, brain imaging technologies, and computational analysis. Researchers began employing functional magnetic resonance imaging (fMRI) and other neuroimaging techniques to explore the neural correlates of lucid dreaming.

These studies revealed fascinating insights into the brain's activities during lucid dreams. For example, researchers identified increased activity in the prefrontal cortex, the region associated with self-awareness and executive functions, during lucid dreaming. This finding provided empirical evidence supporting the notion that lucid dreaming involves conscious awareness and volitional control within the dream state.

Moreover, the development of wearable devices and smartphone applications specifically designed for lucid dream induction and monitoring has empowered individuals to explore and engage with their dream experiences. Techniques such as light and sound stimulation, as well as REM sleep detection algorithms, have become accessible tools for aspiring lucid dreamers.

4. The Emergence of Lucid Dreaming Communities:

In parallel with scientific advancements, the internet age has witnessed the emergence of online communities and forums dedicated to the exploration and sharing of lucid dream experiences. Lucid dreaming enthusiasts from around the world come together to exchange knowledge, techniques, and personal accounts, fostering a vibrant and supportive network of dream explorers.

These communities have not only facilitated the dissemination of information but have also provided a platform for collaborative research projects and the collection of large-scale data on lucid dreaming experiences. The collective efforts of dreamers and researchers have further enriched our understanding of lucid dreaming and its potential applications.

In recent years, the interdisciplinary field of consciousness studies has embraced lucid dreaming as a valuable tool for investigating the nature of subjective experience and the boundaries between waking and dreaming states. Lucid dreaming has become a subject of inquiry not only for psychologists and neuroscientists but also for philosophers, cognitive scientists, and transpersonal researchers.

In conclusion, the journey of lucid dreaming, from ancient accounts and philosophical ponderings to scientific inquiry and technological advancements, has transformed this once-elusive phenomenon into a subject of study and exploration. Through the tireless efforts of countless individuals, lucid dreaming has emerged from the shadows of mystical speculation into the realm of empirical investigation.

As we continue our exploration in this book, drawing upon the historical and scientific foundations laid by those who came before us, we shall venture deeper into the realms of lucid dreaming. We shall unravel the mechanisms, techniques, and transformative potentials that lie within this extraordinary state of consciousness. The discovery of lucid dreaming marks a profound milestone in our understanding of the human mind and its inherent capacity for exploration, growth, and self-discovery within the realm of dreams.

THE NEUROBIOLOGY OF LUCID DREAMING:

The phenomenon of lucid dreaming continues to captivate the scientific community as researchers delve into the intricate neurobiological mechanisms that underlie this unique state of consciousness. In this section, we will embark on a comprehensive exploration of the neurobiology of lucid dreaming, unraveling the brain's activities and processes that give rise to conscious awareness and control within dreams.

1. Prefrontal Cortex and Self-Awareness:

One of the key areas of the brain that has been extensively studied in relation to lucid dreaming is the prefrontal cortex (PFC). This region, located at the front of the brain, is associated with higher-order cognitive functions such as decision-making, self-awareness, and metacognition—the ability to reflect upon and monitor one's own mental processes.

Research using neuroimaging techniques, such as functional magnetic resonance imaging (fMRI), has revealed increased activity in the PFC during lucid dreaming. This heightened activation suggests that the PFC plays a critical role in the experience of lucidity and the ability to maintain self-awareness within dreams.

Furthermore, studies have shown that the dorsolateral prefrontal cortex (DLPFC), a specific area within the PFC, is particularly active during lucid dreaming. The DLPFC is involved in working memory, attention regulation, and cognitive control. Its activation during lucid dreaming suggests that it may contribute to the cognitive processes required for maintaining lucidity and exerting control over dream content.

The involvement of the PFC in lucid dreaming is further supported by research on individuals with PFC damage. Studies have shown that individuals with impaired PFC function are less likely to experience lucid dreams, highlighting the crucial role of this brain region in the phenomenon.

2. REM Sleep and Dream Generation:

Lucid dreaming occurs primarily during the rapid eye movement (REM) stage of sleep, a stage characterized by heightened brain activity and vivid dreams. The neurobiological processes underlying REM sleep play a significant role in the generation of dreams and the potential for conscious awareness within them.

During REM sleep, the brain exhibits patterns of activity that resemble wakefulness, despite the absence of external sensory input. This suggests that the brain generates its own internal representations and simulations, giving rise to the rich and immersive dream experiences that we encounter during REM sleep.

Studies have shown that the visual cortex, responsible for processing visual information, becomes highly active during REM sleep and lucid dreaming. This increased activity contributes to the vividness and realism of dream imagery. Additionally, other brain regions involved in memory consolidation, emotional processing, and sensory integration also exhibit heightened activity during REM sleep, providing a rich neural landscape for the creation of dream narratives.

3. The Role of Neurotransmitters:

Neurotransmitters, the chemical messengers of the brain, play a crucial role in modulating brain activity and influencing the characteristics of different states of consciousness. Several neurotransmitters have been implicated in the neurobiology of lucid dreaming, shedding light on the chemical processes that contribute to the phenomenon.

Acetylcholine, a neurotransmitter involved in cognitive processes and memory formation, has been of particular interest in relation to lucid dreaming. Research suggests that acetylcholine levels are elevated during REM sleep and play a role in facilitating the activation of brain regions associated with visual processing and emotional experiences. The availability of acetylcholine may contribute to the enhanced perceptual clarity and emotional intensity often reported in lucid dreams.

Additionally, the neurotransmitter serotonin has been implicated in the modulation of REM sleep and dream experiences. Serotonin levels fluctuate during sleep, with lower levels observed during REM sleep. Some researchers hypothesize that decreased serotonin levels may create an environment conducive to lucid dreaming by reducing inhibitory control and allowing for increased brain activation and self-awareness within dreams.

4. Emerging Perspectives: From Networks to Oscillations

While the aforementioned findings provide valuable insights into the neurobiology of lucid dreaming, it is important to note that our understanding of this phenomenon is still evolving. Recent advancements in neuroscience have introduced new perspectives and methodologies for investigating the brain's activities during different states of consciousness.

One such perspective is the study of functional connectivity—the network of brain regions that exhibit synchronized activity during specific tasks or states. By examining the patterns of functional connectivity during lucid dreaming, researchers have begun to unravel the dynamic interactions between different brain regions and networks.

Studies using techniques such as electroencephalography (EEG) and functional connectivity analysis have identified distinct patterns of brain connectivity during lucid dreaming. These findings suggest that specific networks, including the default mode network (DMN) involved in self-referential thinking and the frontoparietal network associated with attention and cognitive control, may play a crucial role in maintaining conscious awareness and metacognition within dreams.

Furthermore, investigations into the oscillatory dynamics of the brain have provided valuable insights into the neurobiology of lucid dreaming. Brain oscillations, rhythmic patterns of neural activity, have been associated with different cognitive processes and states of consciousness. Preliminary research suggests that specific oscillatory patterns, such as gamma oscillations, may be enhanced during lucid dreaming, potentially facilitating the integration of information and the coordination of neural networks crucial for lucid awareness.

Finally, the exploration of the neurobiology of lucid dreaming has uncovered remarkable insights into the brain's activities during this extraordinary state of consciousness. The prefrontal cortex, with its involvement in self-awareness and cognitive control, emerges as a key player in the experience of lucidity. The intricate interplay between neurotransmitters, brain networks, and oscillatory dynamics contributes to the generation and modulation of dream experiences.

As our understanding of the neurobiology of lucid dreaming continues to deepen, new avenues for research and applications emerge. From potential therapeutic interventions for mental health conditions to harnessing lucid dreaming for creativity and self-exploration, the exploration of lucid dreaming's neurobiological underpinnings holds immense promise for unlocking the hidden potentials of the human mind within the realm of dreams.

THE ROLE OF DOPAMINE

Dopamine, a neurotransmitter often associated with reward and motivation, has garnered significant interest in the study of lucid dreaming. Its involvement in the brain's reward system and its influence on various cognitive processes make it a compelling candidate for understanding the neurobiology of lucid dreaming. In this section, we will delve into the multifaceted role of dopamine and its potential implications for the phenomenon of lucid dreaming.

1. Dopamine and Reward:

One of the primary functions associated with dopamine is its role in the brain's reward system. Dopamine is released in response to pleasurable experiences, reinforcing behavior and motivating individuals to seek out rewarding stimuli. This reward-based system has been implicated in various aspects of human experience, including motivation, learning, and decision-making.

In the context of lucid dreaming, dopamine may play a crucial role in the reinforcement and maintenance of lucid awareness within dreams. It is hypothesized that the activation of dopaminergic pathways during lucid dreaming can contribute to the rewarding nature of the experience by reinforcing the cognitive processes associated with self-awareness and conscious control.

Studies have suggested a correlation between dopamine and the frequency of lucid dreaming experiences. For instance, individuals with higher levels of dopamine-related genetic markers have been found to report more frequent lucid dreaming. This association hints at the possibility that dopamine levels may influence the propensity to experience lucid dreams, although further research is needed to establish a definitive link.

2. Dopamine and Cognitive Function:

Beyond its role in the reward system, dopamine is also involved in various cognitive functions, including attention, working memory, and cognitive flexibility. These cognitive processes are vital for maintaining lucidity and exerting control over dreams.

Research has shown that dopamine influences attentional processes, enhancing the ability to focus and sustain attention on specific tasks or stimuli. In the context of lucid dreaming, this heightened attentional capacity facilitated by dopamine may contribute to the maintenance of lucid awareness and the ability to engage with the dream environment.

Working memory, the system responsible for the temporary storage and manipulation of information, is another cognitive process that may be influenced by dopamine. Lucid dreaming often requires the ability to hold multiple goals or intentions in mind simultaneously, such as remembering to carry out specific actions or maintaining awareness of the dream state. Dopamine's influence on working memory may enhance these cognitive abilities, aiding in the execution of planned actions and the retention of lucidity within dreams.

Furthermore, dopamine has been implicated in cognitive flexibility—the capacity to adapt and shift between different mental frameworks or perspectives. Lucid dreaming involves the ability to recognize the dream state and exercise control over the dream content. Dopamine's influence on cognitive flexibility may contribute to the capacity to shift between different states of consciousness, enabling individuals to transition into a lucid state and navigate the dream world.

3. Pharmacological Interventions and Dopaminergic Modulation:

Given dopamine's potential role in lucid dreaming, researchers have explored the effects of pharmacological interventions that modulate dopamine levels on dream experiences. One such intervention is the administration of dopamine agonists, which enhance dopamine activity in the brain.

Studies have shown that the administration of dopamine agonists, such as pramipexole or levodopa, can increase the frequency and intensity of lucid dreams in some individuals. These findings suggest that manipulating dopamine levels may indeed influence the likelihood and quality of lucid dreaming experiences.

However, it is important to note that dopamine modulation is a complex process, and its effects on lucid dreaming may vary among individuals. Factors such as baseline dopamine levels, individual differences in dopamine receptor sensitivity, and other neurotransmitter systems' interactions can influence the outcomes of dopamine-modulating interventions.

In conclusion, dopamine, with its involvement in reward, motivation, and cognitive processes, offers intriguing insights into the neurobiology of lucid dreaming. Its role in the brain's reward system may contribute to the reinforcing nature of lucid experiences, while its influence on attention, working memory, and cognitive flexibility may enhance the cognitive abilities required for maintaining lucidity within dreams.

The relationship between dopamine and lucid dreaming is a complex and multifaceted area of research, with many questions yet to be answered. Further studies exploring the interplay between dopamine and other neurotransmitter systems, as well as individual differences in dopaminergic functioning, will contribute to a more comprehensive understanding of the role of dopamine in the phenomenon of lucid dreaming.

THE COGNITIVE AND PSYCHOLOGICAL IMPLICATIONS:

Lucid dreaming is not only a fascinating phenomenon from a neurobiological perspective but also holds profound cognitive and psychological implications. In this section, we will explore the cognitive and psychological aspects of lucid dreaming, shedding light on its potential benefits and applications in various domains of human experience.

1. Enhanced Metacognition and Self-Reflection:

One of the primary cognitive implications of lucid dreaming is its association with enhanced metacognition, which refers to the ability to reflect upon and monitor one's own mental processes. Lucid dreamers exhibit a unique capacity to recognize the dream state and maintain self-awareness within the dream environment.

By becoming aware that they are dreaming, lucid dreamers gain access to a unique platform for self-reflection and self-exploration. They can consciously observe and interact with dream content, explore their inner thoughts, emotions, and desires, and gain insights into their unconscious mind. This heightened metacognitive awareness can extend beyond the dream state, fostering a deeper understanding of one's thoughts, motivations, and personal experiences in waking life.

2. Creative Exploration and Problem Solving:

Lucid dreaming also offers fertile ground for creative exploration and problem-solving. Within lucid dreams, individuals have the freedom to manipulate the dream environment, engage in imaginative activities, and experiment with different possibilities. This creative potential within dreams can extend to artistic pursuits, scientific exploration, and personal development.

Many renowned artists, writers, and inventors have attributed their creative breakthroughs to insights gained through dreams. Lucid dreaming provides a unique avenue for tapping into the wellspring of imagination, allowing individuals to explore unconventional ideas, generate novel solutions, and overcome creative blocks.

Moreover, lucid dreaming can be utilized as a tool for problem-solving and decision-making. By setting intentions before sleep, individuals can direct their dreaming minds to work on specific challenges or questions. Lucid dreams can provide a space for testing hypotheses, visualizing potential outcomes, and gaining new perspectives, ultimately aiding in the resolution of real-life problems.

3. Emotional Regulation and Therapeutic Potential:

Emotions play a significant role in both dreaming and waking life. Lucid dreaming offers a platform for exploring and regulating emotions within the context of dreams, which can have profound psychological implications. Through lucid awareness, individuals can consciously confront and process emotional experiences, gaining insights and facilitating emotional healing.

Lucid dreaming can be particularly beneficial for individuals suffering from recurring nightmares or trauma-related dreams. By becoming aware that they are dreaming, individuals can actively intervene in the dream narrative, transform frightening scenarios, and gain a sense of mastery over their fears. This process, known as lucid dream therapy, has shown promising results in reducing the frequency and intensity of nightmares, providing relief for those experiencing sleep disturbances and related psychological distress.

4. Personal Growth and Self-Actualization:

Lucid dreaming holds immense potential for personal growth and self-actualization. It offers a unique playground for self-exploration, self-expression, and self-development. Through lucid dreams, individuals can confront fears, expand their boundaries, and cultivate qualities such as courage, creativity, and resilience.

Lucid dreaming can also facilitate the exploration of personal goals, aspirations, and values. By setting intentions before sleep, individuals can utilize their lucid dreams as a platform for rehearsing desired behaviors, practicing skills, and visualizing successful outcomes. This process of "dream incubation" can enhance motivation, build confidence, and support the pursuit of personal aspirations in waking life.

5. Spiritual and Transcendent Experiences:

For many individuals, lucid dreaming offers a pathway to spiritual and transcendent experiences. The ability to navigate and manipulate the dream world can provide a sense of profound connectedness, awe, and spiritual exploration. Lucid dreamers report encounters with deceased loved ones, mystical experiences, and a deep sense of interconnectedness with the universe.

These spiritual dimensions of lucid dreaming can inspire individuals to explore questions of meaning, purpose, and the nature of consciousness itself. Lucid dreams can serve as a bridge between the ordinary and the extraordinary, offering glimpses into realms beyond the limitations of everyday experience.

The cognitive and psychological implications of lucid dreaming are vast and multifaceted. From enhanced metacognition and creative exploration to emotional regulation and personal growth, lucid dreaming opens up new realms of possibilities for self-discovery and self-actualization. Its therapeutic potential, problem-solving capabilities, and spiritual dimensions further contribute to its significance as a remarkable state of consciousness. As we continue to unravel the mysteries of lucid dreaming, its cognitive and psychological implications hold immense promise for harnessing the power of the mind and unlocking the potential of human experience.

APPLICATIONS OF LUCID DREAMING RESEARCH:

The exploration of lucid dreaming has not only deepened our understanding of this extraordinary phenomenon but has also paved the way for various practical applications. In this section, we will delve into the diverse applications of lucid dreaming research, ranging from therapeutic interventions to personal development and beyond.

1. Lucid Dream Therapy:

One of the most promising applications of lucid dreaming research is in the fields of therapy and mental health. Lucid dream therapy utilizes the unique properties of lucid dreaming to address psychological issues such as nightmares, phobias, and trauma-related symptoms.

By training individuals to become proficient in lucid dreaming techniques, therapists can empower their clients to confront and transform distressing dream experiences. Through lucid awareness, individuals can actively engage with their dreams, alter negative dream content, and gain a sense of mastery over their fears. This therapeutic approach has shown promising results in reducing nightmare frequency, alleviating sleep disturbances, and promoting psychological well-being.

Furthermore, lucid dreaming research has extended into the realm of post-traumatic stress disorder (PTSD) treatment. Lucid dream therapy, combined with traditional trauma-focused therapies, offers a unique opportunity for individuals to safely process and reframe traumatic experiences within the context of dreams. This approach holds potential for enhancing therapeutic outcomes and promoting post-traumatic growth.

2. Enhancing Creativity and Problem-Solving:

Lucid dreaming has long been recognized as a fertile ground for creative exploration and problem-solving. Artists, writers, and inventors have utilized lucid dreaming as a source of inspiration and insight throughout history. Recent research has begun to uncover the mechanisms underlying these creative benefits and explore practical applications.

By intentionally setting intentions before sleep, individuals can direct their dreaming minds toward specific creative challenges or problem-solving tasks. Lucid dreams provide a platform for experimentation, visualizing solutions, and generating innovative ideas. This approach has been utilized in fields such as design, engineering, and scientific research to spark novel perspectives and breakthrough innovations.

3. Skill Enhancement and Practice:

Lucid dreaming can be utilized as a tool for skill enhancement and practice. Through lucid dreams, individuals can engage in mental rehearsal and simulate desired behaviors, improving performance in various domains.

Athletes, musicians, and performers have leveraged lucid dreaming to refine their skills, overcome performance anxiety, and visualize successful outcomes. By rehearsing complex movements, perfecting techniques, and experiencing the sensations associated with their craft, individuals can enhance their abilities in waking life.

4. Personal Development and Self-Exploration:

Lucid dreaming holds immense potential for personal development and self-exploration. By consciously navigating the dream world, individuals can delve into the depths of their unconscious mind, confront fears and limiting beliefs, and gain insights into their personal growth journey.

Lucid dreams offer a unique platform for exploring aspects of the self, including identity, values, and aspirations. Individuals can engage in inner dialogue, seek guidance from dream characters, and gain a deeper understanding of their desires and motivations. Lucid dreaming can facilitate self-reflection, promote introspection, and support personal transformation.

5. Transcendental and Spiritual Experiences:

Lucid dreaming research has shed light on the potential for transcendental and spiritual experiences within dreams. These experiences can provide individuals with a profound sense of connectedness, meaning, and spiritual exploration.

Through lucid dreams, individuals report encounters with deceased loved ones, mystical insights, and experiences of expanded consciousness. These experiences have implications for the study of consciousness, the nature of reality, and the exploration of spiritual dimensions.

6. Education and Learning:

Lucid dreaming research has implications for education and learning. The ability to consciously engage with dream content opens up possibilities for enhancing memory, creativity, and knowledge acquisition.

Lucid dreaming can be used as a platform for immersive learning experiences, allowing individuals to explore historical events, scientific concepts, or cultural phenomena within the dream state. By intentionally setting intentions to learn during lucid dreams, individuals can enhance memory consolidation, stimulate creativity, and deepen their understanding of complex subjects.

In conclusion, the applications of lucid dreaming research are vast and diverse, spanning fields such as therapy, creativity, personal development, and education. As our understanding of lucid dreaming continues to evolve, these applications hold the potential to transform various aspects of human experience. From alleviating psychological distress to unlocking creative potential and fostering personal growth, the practical implications of lucid dreaming research are wide-ranging and offer exciting possibilities for harnessing the power of the dream state.

CONCLUSION

As our understanding of the science behind lucid dreaming deepens, we continue to unravel the mysteries of the mind. Through neurobiological research, we have discovered the unique brain activities associated with lucid dreaming, shedding light on its nature and potential applications. The cognitive and psychological implications are vast, offering exciting possibilities for personal growth, creativity, and therapeutic interventions.

In the next chapter, we will delve into the realm of dream interpretation, exploring how lucid dreaming can enhance our understanding of the symbolism and meaning behind our dreams. Prepare to unlock the secrets hidden within your nocturnal adventures as we embark on a journey of self-discovery and exploration.

CHAPTER 3

Dream Interpretation

INTRODUCTION

Dreams have always held a mysterious allure, captivating human curiosity and imagination. Throughout history, they have been regarded as portals to the subconscious, gateways to hidden realms, and windows into the depths of the human psyche. From the ancient civilizations of Egypt, Greece, and China to the modern explorations of Freud and Jung, dream interpretation has been a prominent practice that seeks to unravel the enigmatic messages concealed within our dreams. In this chapter, we embark on a captivating journey into the realm of dream interpretation, exploring how the practice of lucid dreaming can enhance our understanding of these ethereal experiences and unveil the profound insights they offer.

Dreams, those ephemeral landscapes of the mind, have fascinated and perplexed humanity since time immemorial. As we close our eyes and surrender to sleep, our minds embark on extraordinary voyages, weaving tapestries of experiences, emotions, and imagery that seem both familiar and utterly foreign. Dreams can transport us to alternate realities, rekindle forgotten memories, evoke intense emotions, and bring forth the unspoken desires lurking beneath our conscious awareness. They possess a language all their own, communicating with us through a rich tapestry of symbols, metaphors, and surreal landscapes.

But what are dreams, and why do they hold such fascination for us? Dreams are the creations of our subconscious minds, a realm where our deepest fears, desires, conflicts, and aspirations converge. They are the residue of our waking experiences, interwoven with fragments of memories, emotions, and the collective wisdom of humanity. Dreams can be both cryptic and revelatory, speaking to us in a language that defies logic and linear thinking. In the realm of dreams, the laws of physics give way to boundless possibilities, and the limitations of our physical existence dissolve into the ethereal.

Dream interpretation, the art of deciphering the meaning hidden within dreams, is a practice that has spanned cultures and generations. Ancient civilizations, recognizing the significance of dreams, attributed them to divine messages, spiritual encounters, or glimpses into other dimensions. The Egyptians, for instance, believed that dreams were a conduit between the mortal and divine realms, often seeking guidance from dreams in matters of life, death, and destiny. The Greeks, too, held dreams in high esteem, with figures like Artemidorus and Plato delving into the complexities of dream symbolism and meaning.

In the modern era, dream interpretation underwent a transformative shift with the groundbreaking work of Sigmund Freud and Carl Jung. Freud, the father of psychoanalysis, viewed dreams as the "royal road to the unconscious," peering into the hidden recesses of the mind. He believed that dreams were symbolic representations of repressed desires and unresolved conflicts, offering a pathway to unveil the secret workings of the human psyche. Jung, on the other hand, expanded upon Freud's ideas, delving into the collective unconscious and the archetypal imagery that permeates our dreams. For Jung, dreams were a portal to the shared wisdom and universal truths embedded within the human collective.

The essence of dream interpretation lies in understanding the symbolic language of dreams. Dreams speak to us through a rich tapestry of symbols, metaphors, and archetypal imagery, transcending the limitations of spoken language. Each symbol carries a multitude of meanings, influenced by personal associations, cultural contexts, and universal archetypes. The interpretation of dreams is not a rigid science but a deeply personal and intuitive endeavor. It requires delving into the depths of our own subconscious, exploring the emotional resonance of dream elements, and unraveling the hidden threads that connect them.

To embark on the journey of dream interpretation, it is crucial to develop a keen awareness of the elements that populate our dreams. Dreams are composed of various elements, such as people, objects, locations, actions, and emotions, each offering a glimpse into the hidden recesses of our minds. These elements can be viewed as pieces of a puzzle—fragments of our waking experiences that have been reshaped and recontextualized by the subconscious. By unraveling the threads that connect these elements, we can unravel the underlying messages and insights they hold.

Keeping a dream journal is a vital tool for dream interpretation. The act of recording our dreams immediately upon waking allows us to capture the fleeting details, emotions, and sensations that may otherwise fade from memory. A dream journal serves as a chronicle of our dream journeys and a repository of experiences that can be revisited and analyzed. As we reflect upon our dreams over time, patterns and recurring themes may emerge, unveiling the hidden symbolism and overarching narratives that shape our dreamscapes.

As we delve deeper into the realm of dream interpretation, we encounter the phenomenon of lucid dreaming—an extraordinary state of consciousness where we become aware that we are dreaming while still immersed in the dream. Lucid dreaming offers a unique opportunity to actively engage in and shape our dreams, transforming them into lucid canvases for exploration and self-discovery.

When we enter a lucid dream, we step into the realm of the alchemist, where the boundaries of reality and imagination blur and the subconscious mind becomes a vast playground of endless potential.

Lucid dreaming opens a gateway to enhanced dream interpretation. By cultivating the skill of lucidity within dreams, we gain the ability to question dream elements, interact with dream characters, and seek profound insights into our own subconscious minds. We become active participants in the dream narrative, shaping and directing its course. Lucid dreaming provides a heightened state of self-awareness, enabling us to navigate the depths of our dreams with intention, curiosity, and a quest for self-discovery.

In this chapter, we embark on a transformative journey into the realm of dream interpretation, guided by the practice of lucid dreaming. We will explore various techniques for dream analysis, from deciphering symbolic imagery to engaging in dialogue with dream characters. We will learn how to keep a dream journal as a powerful tool for reflection and exploration. Through the practice of lucid dreaming, we will unlock the hidden messages and profound insights embedded within our dreams, illuminating the paths to personal growth, self-discovery, and a deeper connection with our inner selves.

Join us as we embark on this captivating exploration of dream interpretation, unraveling the mysteries that lie within our dreams, and embarking on a transformative journey into the depths of the human subconscious. Prepare to awaken to the hidden wisdom of your dreams, for within them lies the key to unlocking the secrets of your innermost self.

THE NATURE OF DREAMS

Dreams, those ethereal manifestations of the mind, captivate us with their enigmatic nature and their ability to transport us to extraordinary realms. To truly delve into the practice of dream interpretation, it is essential to understand the multifaceted and intricate nature of dreams themselves. In this section, we embark on an immersive exploration of the nature of dreams, unraveling their mysteries and shedding light on the profound experiences that unfold within the realm of slumber.

When we close our eyes and surrender to sleep, we enter a realm where the boundaries of reality are blurred and the limitations of our physical existence fade away. Dreams are the manifestations of our subconscious minds, the product of a complex interplay of thoughts, emotions, memories, and desires that arise as we slumber. They serve as a bridge between the conscious and unconscious realms, offering us glimpses into the depths of our psyche and the hidden realms of our innermost selves.

The experience of dreaming is as diverse as the individuals who engage in it. Dreams can be vivid and lifelike, brimming with sensory impressions that mimic our waking reality. They can also be fragmented, disjointed narratives that jump from one scene to another with no apparent logic. Dreams may be pleasant and serene, filled with joy and tranquility, or they can be fraught with tension, fear, and anxiety, evoking a whirlwind of emotions that linger even upon waking.

The content of dreams is as vast and varied as the human experience itself. Dreams can take us on thrilling adventures where we soar through the skies, explore uncharted landscapes, and interact with fantastical creatures. They can transport us to long-forgotten memories, reliving moments from our past with startling clarity. Dreams may also confront us with our deepest fears and insecurities, presenting us with symbolic challenges and puzzles that beckon us to uncover their hidden meanings.

Dreams possess a language all their own—a language of symbols, metaphors, and imagery that bypasses the constraints of rational thought and linear storytelling. The subconscious mind communicates through a rich tapestry of symbols, weaving together archetypal figures, familiar faces, and enigmatic landscapes to convey deeper truths and insights. These symbols are deeply personal, drawing upon our individual experiences, memories, and cultural backgrounds. Yet they can also tap into the collective unconscious—the shared reservoir of human experience and wisdom that transcends time and space.

Symbolism in dreams is a cornerstone of dream interpretation. Each symbol carries a multitude of meanings, influenced by personal associations, cultural contexts, and universal archetypes. For instance, a snake in a dream can symbolize transformation, healing, or even deceit, depending on the individual's personal experiences and cultural beliefs. Similarly, water can represent purification, emotional depths, or the ebb and flow of life's cycles. Unraveling these symbols and deciphering their meanings is a crucial aspect of dream interpretation.

While dreams often seem elusive and fleeting, they possess a remarkable ability to leave a lasting impression on our waking consciousness. The emotions we experience within dreams—whether joy, fear, love, or sorrow—can linger long after we wake, influencing our mood, thoughts, and actions. Dreams have the power to ignite our creativity, spark new insights, and provide us with a fresh perspective on waking life. They offer us a window into the unexplored recesses of our minds, inviting us to engage in introspection, self-reflection, and personal growth.

Dreams also serve as a means of processing and integrating our daily experiences. They act as a theater for the mind, where we can replay, reframe, and make sense of the events, emotions, and challenges we encounter in our waking lives. Dreams allow us to process unresolved conflicts, confront buried traumas, and explore the depths of our desires and aspirations. They provide a safe space for the subconscious mind to explore, experiment, and communicate with the conscious self.

Throughout history, cultures across the globe have attributed significance to dreams, recognizing their potential for divination, spiritual revelation, and personal guidance. Ancient civilizations sought counsel from dreams, seeking guidance from the gods, or using dreams as a tool for prophecy. Indigenous cultures viewed dreams as a sacred conduit to the spirit world, a means of connecting with ancestors and receiving wisdom from the divine. The practice of dream interpretation has been woven into the fabric of human existence, reflecting our innate desire to make sense of the mysteries that unfold in the realm of sleep.

In the modern era, the field of psychology has shed new light on the nature and function of dreams. Pioneers like Sigmund Freud and Carl Jung brought forth groundbreaking theories that revolutionized our understanding of dreams and their interpretation. Freud's psychoanalytic perspective emphasized the role of dreams in revealing repressed desires, unresolved conflicts, and unconscious motivations. He believed that dreams provided a pathway for the subconscious mind to express forbidden or socially unacceptable thoughts and wishes.

Jung, on the other hand, expanded upon Freud's theories and delved into the collective unconscious—a vast reservoir of shared archetypes and universal symbols that underpin the human experience. For Jung, dreams served as a means of accessing this collective wisdom, offering insights into our individual and collective journeys of self-discovery and personal growth. According to Jung, dreams provided a symbolic language through which the unconscious could communicate with the conscious mind, leading to the integration of hidden aspects of the self.

As we explore the nature of dreams, it becomes evident that dreams are not isolated fragments of the mind but intricate narratives that interweave with our waking lives. They reflect our deepest desires, fears, hopes, and aspirations, serving as a mirror that reveals the innermost workings of our subconscious minds. Dreams can be regarded as the voice of our intuition, our inner guide, offering us glimpses of untapped potential, unhealed wounds, and unexplored territories within ourselves.

The beauty of dream interpretation lies in its capacity to uncover the hidden treasures buried within our dreams. By engaging in the practice of dream analysis, we embark on a journey of self-discovery and self-awareness. We learn to decipher the language of symbols, to explore the intricate threads that connect dream elements, and to unveil the underlying messages that guide our subconscious minds. Through the exploration of dreams, we gain insight into our fears, desires, and conflicts, fostering personal growth, healing, and a deeper understanding of ourselves.

In the following sections of this chapter, we will delve into the techniques and tools of dream interpretation. We will explore how lucid dreaming can enhance our ability to decipher dream symbolism and engage in meaningful dialogues with dream characters. We will learn how to use a dream journal as a powerful tool for reflection and self-analysis.

Together, we will embark on a transformative journey into the realm of dream interpretation, unlocking the profound wisdom and insights that lie within our dreams.

As we unravel the mysteries of our dreams, we open ourselves to a deeper understanding of the self, an expanded awareness of our inner landscape, and a heightened connection with the boundless realms of the subconscious. Prepare to embark on a voyage into the heart of your dreams, for within them lies the key to unlocking the secrets of your soul.

THE HISTORY OF DREAM INTERPRETATION

Dreams have fascinated and intrigued humanity since time immemorial. Across cultures and civilizations, dreams have been regarded as powerful sources of insight, prophecy, and spiritual guidance. The practice of interpreting dreams dates back to ancient times, when dreams were seen as a bridge between the earthly realm and the divine. In this section, we delve into the rich tapestry of the history of dream interpretation, exploring the beliefs, theories, and practices that have shaped our understanding of dreams throughout the ages.

Ancient civilizations viewed dreams with great reverence, considering them to be direct messages from the gods or the spirit world. In Mesopotamia, dreams held immense significance, and dream interpreters were revered as sacred figures who could unlock the mysteries of the divine realm. The Babylonians, for instance, documented their dreams on clay tablets and consulted dream oracles to gain insights into matters of personal and societal importance. Similarly, the Egyptians believed that dreams were messages from the gods and utilized dream interpretation as a means of guidance and prophecy.

The practice of dream interpretation also held a prominent place in ancient Greece. The Greeks attributed great importance to dreams, seeing them as visitations from the gods or as reflections of the dreamer's own subconscious mind. The influential philosopher and mathematician Pythagoras believed that dreams contained hidden truths and sought to unravel their meanings. His disciple, Plato, considered dreams to be symbolic representations of the soul's journey and explored their significance in his dialogues.

In the realm of ancient religions, dreams played a central role. The Hebrew Bible, for instance, abounds with stories of prophetic dreams, where divine messages and guidance were conveyed through vivid and symbolic dream experiences. The story of Joseph in the Book of Genesis serves as a prime example, where Joseph's dreams foretold his rise to power and became a pivotal factor in the unfolding of events.

Similarly, in Hinduism, dreams were seen as divine revelations, with the sacred text Rigveda containing references to dream interpretation as a means of accessing spiritual knowledge.

Dream interpretation also found its place in the teachings of renowned philosophers and scholars throughout history. In the Hellenistic period, the Greek philosopher Aristotle pondered the nature and meaning of dreams, proposing theories that linked dreams to physiological and psychological processes. His work influenced later scholars and philosophers, contributing to the development of theories regarding the function and interpretation of dreams.

The Middle Ages witnessed a shift in the perception of dreams as religious interpretations took precedence. Dreams were seen as battlegrounds for the forces of good and evil, where spiritual beings, such as angels and demons, engaged in cosmic struggles. Dream interpretation during this period was heavily influenced by Christian theology and often focused on discerning the divine will and avoiding sinful temptations.

One of the most influential figures in the history of dream interpretation is Sigmund Freud, the father of psychoanalysis. In the late 19th and early 20th centuries, Freud revolutionized the field of psychology by introducing a groundbreaking theory on the interpretation of dreams. Freud believed that dreams were a manifestation of repressed desires and unconscious conflicts, offering a pathway for the expression of forbidden or socially unacceptable thoughts and wishes.

According to Freud's psychoanalytic theory, dreams were symbolic representations of unconscious desires and wishes that were disguised and distorted to protect the dreamer from the anxiety they might provoke. Freud developed techniques such as free association and dream analysis to uncover the hidden meanings embedded within dreams. He believed that by unraveling the symbolism and latent content of dreams, individuals could gain insight into their deepest motivations and psychological states.

Freud's theories sparked a surge of interest in dream interpretation, influencing not only the field of psychology but also popular culture. His ideas brought the exploration of dreams into the mainstream, encouraging individuals to examine their dreams as a means of self-discovery and understanding. However, Freud's focus on sexual and aggressive instincts as the driving forces behind dreams has been subject to criticism and has led to the development of alternative theories and approaches to dream interpretation.

Carl Jung, a Swiss psychiatrist and influential figure in the field of analytical psychology, offered an alternative perspective on dream interpretation. Jung expanded upon Freud's theories, emphasizing the importance of the collective unconscious—a shared reservoir of archetypes and universal symbols that underpin the human experience. He believed that dreams provided a means of accessing this collective wisdom, offering insights into our individual and collective journeys of self-discovery and personal growth.

Jung regarded dreams as a reflection of the psyche's attempt to achieve wholeness and balance, incorporating both personal and universal symbols. He introduced the concept of "individuation," the process of integrating hidden aspects of the self through self-reflection and self-awareness. Jungian dream interpretation focused on the exploration of archetypal symbols and their meaning within the individual's personal and cultural context.

Dream interpretation continues to evolve and adapt in modern times. With advancements in neuroscience and the understanding of the brain's functioning during sleep, scientific research has shed new light on the physiological and cognitive processes underlying dreams. While the scientific approach focuses primarily on the mechanisms of dreaming rather than the subjective interpretation of dream content, it has contributed valuable insights into the understanding of dreams and their connection to waking life.

Today, various approaches to dream interpretation coexist, drawing from psychological, spiritual, and cultural perspectives. Some individuals approach dream analysis from a psychological standpoint, using techniques such as journaling, association, and exploration of dream symbols to gain self-awareness and insight. Others find meaning in dreams through spiritual or metaphysical lenses, interpreting them as messages from higher realms or the subconscious mind.

As we explore the history of dream interpretation, we witness the evolution of our understanding of dreams and their significance in the human experience. Dreams have transcended time, cultures, and belief systems, leaving an indelible mark on our collective consciousness. The practice of dream interpretation continues to be a source of fascination, providing a glimpse into the depths of the human psyche and offering a pathway to self-discovery, personal growth, and a deeper connection with the mysteries of the dream world.

UNDERSTANDING SYMBOLISM IN DREAMS

Dreams have long been recognized as a realm where symbolism reigns supreme. The images, objects, and scenarios that unfold within our dreams often carry deeper meanings and messages that can be deciphered through an understanding of dream symbolism. In this section, we embark on a journey into the intricate world of symbolism in dreams, exploring the ways in which symbols manifest, their significance, and the techniques for unraveling their hidden messages.

Symbolism is a language of the subconscious mind, a means of communication that bypasses the constraints of logic and linear thinking. In dreams, symbols serve as a bridge between the conscious and unconscious realms, carrying profound insights and revelations. Dreams often present themselves in symbolic form, employing vivid and sometimes surreal imagery to convey deeper emotions, desires, fears, or conflicts that may be operating beneath the surface of our conscious awareness.

The interpretation of dream symbols requires a nuanced understanding of their context and personal significance. While certain symbols may hold universal meanings across cultures and time, the interpretation of symbols in dreams is highly subjective and influenced by personal experiences, beliefs, and cultural background. What may symbolize love for one person could represent fear or loss for another. Therefore, it is crucial to approach dream symbolism with an open and curious mind, recognizing the unique symbolism that unfolds within our individual dreamscapes.

To navigate the vast landscape of dream symbolism, it is helpful to familiarize ourselves with common archetypal symbols that frequently appear in dreams. Archetypes are universal patterns or themes that are deeply ingrained in the collective unconscious, transcending cultural boundaries. These archetypal symbols, such as water, animals, or houses, carry inherent meanings that tap into shared human experiences and emotions.

Water, for example, often symbolizes the realm of the unconscious, emotions, and the flow of life. It can represent purification, renewal, or the depths of the psyche. Animals, on the other hand, may embody specific qualities or characteristics associated with them. A lion might symbolize strength, courage, or leadership, while a snake can represent transformation, healing, or hidden knowledge.

While archetypal symbols provide a foundation for understanding dream symbolism, it is crucial to consider the personal associations and experiences connected to specific symbols. For instance, a rose may hold different meanings for someone who associates it with love and beauty compared to someone who sees it as a reminder of loss or betrayal. Personal experiences, memories, and cultural influences shape our individual interpretations of symbols, adding depth and complexity to the dream landscape.

The process of interpreting dream symbols involves both intuitive exploration and conscious reflection. It is essential to approach symbols with curiosity and openness, allowing their meanings to unfold organically. One effective technique for exploring dream symbolism is free association. By examining the emotional reactions, memories, and thoughts that arise when contemplating a specific symbol, we can unravel the personal significance it holds for us.

Dream journals are valuable tools for recording and reflecting on dream symbolism. By writing down dreams and noting the symbols, emotions, and experiences associated with them, we create a treasure trove of material for interpretation. Over time, patterns and recurring symbols may emerge, providing valuable insights into our inner world and the themes that occupy our subconscious mind.

Another approach to understanding dream symbolism is active imagination. This technique, pioneered by Carl Jung, involves engaging with dream images through imagination and contemplation. By immersing oneself in the symbol, allowing it to come to life within the mind, and engaging in a dialogue or exploration of its meaning, we can gain deeper insights into its significance for our personal journey.

Dream symbolism is not limited to individual symbols but also encompasses the relationships and interactions between symbols within a dream. The overall narrative, the sequence of events, and the connections between symbols all contribute to the dream's holistic meaning. Analyzing these elements in conjunction with individual symbols can provide a more comprehensive understanding of the messages and themes embedded in the dream.

It is crucial to approach dream interpretation with a sense of curiosity, respect, and humility. Dreams are highly personal and often reflect our deepest desires, fears, and unresolved conflicts. While dream symbolism offers a window into the unconscious, it is essential to remember that dreams are not mere puzzles to be solved but rather invitations to self-exploration and growth.

As we delve into the realm of dream symbolism, we embark on a journey of self-discovery and revelation. Through understanding and interpreting the symbols that populate our dreams, we unlock the hidden messages, emotions, and experiences that shape our waking lives. Dream symbolism serves as a powerful tool for introspection, offering a pathway to self-understanding, personal transformation, and a deeper connection with the intricate workings of our inner world.

ANALYZING DREAM ELEMENTS

Dreams are complex tapestries woven with various elements, including settings, characters, emotions, and actions. Each element contributes to the overall narrative and symbolism of the dream, offering valuable clues and insights into our subconscious mind. In this section, we embark on a detailed exploration of analyzing dream elements, unraveling their meanings, and understanding how they shape the messages conveyed in our dreams.

1. **Settings:**

The settings in dreams provide the backdrop against which the dream unfolds. They can range from familiar places to entirely fantastical or surreal environments. Analyzing dream settings involves considering both their literal and symbolic implications. Familiar locations may represent aspects of our waking lives, while unfamiliar or otherworldly settings may signify unexplored territory within our psyche or represent a symbolic journey.

For example, dreaming of a childhood home could evoke feelings of nostalgia or symbolize a desire to reconnect with aspects of our past. Dreaming of being in a crowded marketplace might reflect a sense of overwhelm or a need to navigate social interactions. Exploring the emotional tone, details, and personal associations connected to dream settings can provide valuable insights into the dream's meaning.

2. **Characters:**

Characters in dreams can take various forms, ranging from known individuals to strangers or even symbolic representations. Analyzing dream characters involves considering their roles, relationships, and the emotions they evoke. Paying attention to how we interact with dream characters and the dynamics that unfold can provide valuable insights into our relationships, unresolved conflicts, or unexpressed emotions.

Dream characters may represent different aspects of ourselves, embodying qualities or traits we associate with them. They can serve as mirrors, teachers, or challengers, helping us navigate the complexities of our inner world. Exploring the interactions, dialogue, and emotional responses evoked by dream characters can shed light on our internal dynamics and provide opportunities for self-reflection and growth.

3. Emotions:

Emotions experienced in dreams carry significant weight and often reflect our subconscious desires, fears, or unresolved emotions. Analyzing the emotional tone of a dream involves identifying the primary emotions present and exploring their underlying causes or triggers. Dreams can evoke a wide range of emotions, from joy and excitement to fear, sadness, and anger.

Exploring the emotions within dreams requires delving deeper into the context and events that elicit these emotional responses. For example, feeling fear in a dream may indicate underlying anxiety or a need to confront unresolved fears in waking life. Joyful or exhilarating emotions within a dream may signify a sense of fulfillment or the pursuit of passions and desires. Understanding the emotional landscape of dreams allows us to gain a deeper understanding of our subconscious desires, conflicts, and emotional well-being.

4. Actions and Events:

The actions and events that unfold within dreams provide important clues to their meaning and symbolism. Analyzing dream actions involves examining the sequence of events, the choices made, and the consequences that arise. Dreams often present scenarios that mirror real-life situations or symbolically represent inner conflicts or desires.

For instance, dreaming of flying might indicate a sense of freedom, empowerment, or a desire to escape constraints. Falling in love in a dream may symbolize a lack of control, insecurity, or a fear of failure. Exploring the actions and events within dreams allows us to uncover hidden narratives, identify patterns, and gain insight into the challenges, aspirations, or unresolved issues that shape our subconscious mind.

5. Symbols:

Symbols within dreams are rich sources of meaning and are often the focal point of dream interpretation. Symbols can take various forms, including objects, animals, colors, or numbers. Analyzing dream symbols involves exploring their personal associations, cultural significance, and archetypal meanings.

Symbols can have both universal and personal interpretations. While certain symbols may carry collective meanings, such as the symbol of a snake representing transformation, personal associations and experiences influence their specific significance within an individual's dream. For example, a red rose might symbolize love and passion for one person, while for another, it may evoke memories of a lost love or symbolize beauty.

To analyze dream symbols effectively, it is important to consider their context within the dream, the emotions they evoke, and any personal connections or associations. Reflecting on the underlying messages, desires, fears, or unresolved issues that symbols represent allows for a deeper understanding of the dream's symbolic language.

In conclusion, analyzing dream elements is a multifaceted process that requires attentiveness, introspection, and an understanding of the interconnectedness of various elements within the dream. By delving into the settings, characters, emotions, actions, and symbols present in our dreams, we unravel the intricate messages embedded within our subconscious mind. Through careful analysis and interpretation, we gain valuable insights into ourselves, our relationships, and the inner forces that shape our waking lives. Dream analysis becomes a powerful tool for self-discovery, personal growth, and the exploration of the profound mysteries of the dream world.

KEEPING A DREAM JOURNAL

Dreams are ephemeral and easily forgotten. Upon waking, the vivid imagery, intricate narratives, and profound emotions that unfolded during the night can quickly slip from our conscious awareness. However, by keeping a dream journal, we can capture and preserve these fleeting moments, unlocking the treasure trove of wisdom and insight that dreams hold. In this section, we delve into the practice of keeping a dream journal, exploring its benefits, techniques, and tips for maximizing its effectiveness.

1. The Importance of a Dream Journal:

A dream journal serves as a dedicated space to record and reflect on our dreams. It provides a tangible record of our dream experiences, enabling us to revisit and analyze them at a later time. The act of recording dreams helps to bridge the gap between the conscious and unconscious minds, fostering a deeper connection with our dream world and the messages it holds.

By maintaining a dream journal, we honor the significance of our dreams and acknowledge their role in our personal growth and self-discovery. Dream journals offer a means of capturing the elusive nature of dreams, allowing us to explore their symbolism, patterns, and themes. They become invaluable tools for unraveling the mysteries of our subconscious mind and gaining a deeper understanding of ourselves.

2. Techniques for Keeping a Dream Journal:

- **Keep the journal by your bedside:** Place your dream journal and a pen or pencil within easy reach of your bed. This practice helps ensure that you can quickly jot down your dreams upon waking, capturing them before they fade from memory.
- **Write immediately upon waking:** As soon as you wake up, take a few moments to reflect on your dreams and begin writing them down. The longer you wait, the more likely you are to forget the details and nuances of your dream experiences.

- **Use keywords and bullet points:** Not every aspect of a dream needs to be fully articulated. Using keywords, phrases, or bullet points can be a quick and effective way to capture the essential elements of the dream without getting caught up in excessive detail.
- **Include emotions and sensations:** In addition to recording the events and imagery of the dream, make note of the emotions and physical sensations you experienced during the dream. Emotions provide valuable insights into the underlying themes and significance of the dream.
- **Draw or sketch:** If you feel inclined, incorporate visual elements into your dream journal. Drawing or sketching specific images or symbols from your dreams can enhance your understanding of their meaning and add a visual dimension to your journaling practice.
- **Reflect and analyze:** After recording your dreams, set aside time to reflect on their potential meanings and messages. Consider the symbols, emotions, and themes that emerged and explore their connections to your waking life. Reflective analysis deepens your engagement with

the dream material and facilitates greater self-awareness.

3. **Maximizing the Effectiveness of Your Dream Journal:**

    - **Consistency is key:** aim to write in your dream journal regularly, ideally immediately upon waking. Consistent journaling helps train your mind to retain dream memories and strengthens your overall dream recall.
    - **Review and revisit:** Periodically review your dream journal entries to identify patterns, recurring symbols, or themes. Pay attention to the connections between different dreams and their potential significance. Reviewing past entries allows for a broader perspective on your dreams and aids in uncovering deeper insights.
    - **Engage in active dream exploration:** Use your dream journal as a starting point for further exploration. Engage in practices such as dream visualization, active imagination, or lucid dreaming techniques to deepen your understanding and interaction with your dreams.
    - **Seek external perspectives:** Consider sharing your dreams with trusted friends, dream groups, or online dream

communities. Discussing and receiving feedback on your dreams from others can provide fresh insights and alternative perspectives on their meaning.

- **Cultivate a receptive mindset:** Approach your dream journaling practice with an open and receptive mindset. Be willing to explore the symbolic language of dreams, embrace the unexpected, and trust in the wisdom that emerges from your subconscious mind.

4. Integrating Dream Journaling into Daily Life:

Dream journaling is not an isolated activity but rather a gateway to a deeper exploration of oneself. Integrating the insights gained from your dream journal into your daily life can enhance personal growth and self-awareness.

- **Reflect on waking life connections:** As you review your dream journal entries, look for connections between your dreams and your waking life experiences. Consider how the symbolism, emotions, or themes in your dreams relate to your thoughts, feelings, or challenges in your everyday life.
- **Set intentions before sleep:** Before going to bed, set an intention to remember your

dreams and gain insights from them. This simple act can prime your subconscious mind to prioritize dream recall and facilitate meaningful dream experiences.

- **Practice gratitude:** express gratitude for the wisdom and guidance received through your dreams. Cultivating an attitude of appreciation and respect for your dream experiences strengthens the bond between your conscious and unconscious minds.
- **Take inspired action:** If your dreams reveal messages or insights that resonate strongly with you, consider taking inspired action in your waking life. Dreams can provide guidance, solutions, or creative inspiration. Act upon the wisdom gained from your dreams to manifest positive change in your life.

In conclusion, keeping a dream journal is a powerful tool for unlocking the depths of our dreams and accessing the profound wisdom they offer. By dedicating time and attention to recording, analyzing, and reflecting upon our dreams, we deepen our understanding of ourselves, foster personal growth, and cultivate a richer connection with our subconscious mind. A dream journal becomes a cherished companion on our journey of self-exploration, serving as a gateway to the transformative power of our dreams.

LUCID DREAMING AND DREAM INTERPRETATION

Lucid dreaming, the state of being aware that one is dreaming while in the midst of a dream, has a unique relationship with dream interpretation. In this section, we explore the intersection between lucid dreaming and dream interpretation, highlighting how lucid dreams can enhance our understanding of the symbolic language of dreams and offer profound opportunities for self-exploration and personal growth.

5. Lucid Dreaming: A Gateway to Dream Interpretation:

Lucid dreaming provides a powerful platform for engaging with and deciphering the symbols and messages within our dreams. When we become lucid within a dream, we gain an extraordinary level of self-awareness and control over the dream narrative. This heightened consciousness allows us to actively explore and interact with the dream environment, including its symbols and symbolism.

- **Symbolic exploration:** Lucid dreaming offers the unique ability to consciously engage with dream symbols. By becoming aware that we are dreaming, we can intentionally seek out specific symbols or evoke their presence within the dream. This deliberate interaction with symbols provides an opportunity for a deeper understanding of their personal significance and expands our capacity for dream interpretation.
- **Real-time analysis:** In a lucid dream, we can analyze and interpret the symbols and events as they unfold, providing immediate insights into their meaning. This real-time analysis allows us to experiment with different interpretations, test hypotheses, and gain a firsthand understanding of the connections between symbols and personal experiences.
- **Direct communication:** Lucid dreaming also opens avenues for direct communication with dream characters or dream figures. Engaging in dialogue with dream characters can provide further clarity and context for the symbolism within the dream. By asking questions, seeking guidance, or requesting explanations from dream characters, we can tap into the

collective wisdom of our subconscious mind.

6. Using Lucid Dreams for Symbolic Integration:

Lucid dreams not only enhance our ability to interpret dreams but also facilitate the integration of dream symbolism into our waking lives. The lucid dream state acts as a bridge between the conscious and unconscious minds, enabling us to bring the insights and wisdom gained from dream symbolism into our daily reality.

- **Dream incubation:** With lucid dreaming, we can consciously set intentions before sleep, requesting specific dreams or insights related to our waking life concerns. This process, known as dream incubation, allows us to explore and receive guidance on specific topics or challenges through dream symbolism.
- **Symbolic embodiment:** In a lucid dream, we have the opportunity to embody and fully experience the symbolism presented. By actively engaging with symbols within the dream, we can gain a deeper understanding of their emotional resonance and the personal significance they hold for us. This embodied experience enriches our

interpretation of dream symbolism and facilitates a more profound integration of its meaning.

- **Dream-inspired actions:** Lucid dreams can inspire actions in our waking lives based on the symbolism and messages encountered within the dream. By translating the insights gained from lucid dreams into practical steps, we can apply the wisdom of the dream world to our daily lives, fostering personal growth and transformation.

7. Ethical Considerations in Lucid Dreaming and Dream Interpretation:

While lucid dreaming enhances dream interpretation, it is essential to approach this practice with ethical considerations in mind. Respecting the boundaries of the dream world, as well as our own and others' autonomy, ensures a responsible and meaningful exploration of dream symbolism.

- **Consent and boundaries:** When engaging with dream characters or dream figures in a lucid dream, it is crucial to respect their autonomy and seek their consent before initiating interactions or interpretations. Honoring the boundaries of the dream world fosters a respectful and ethical approach to dream interpretation.

- **Personal reflection and growth:** Lucid dreaming should not be used solely for personal gain or manipulation of dream symbols. Instead, it should be viewed as a tool for personal reflection, self-discovery, and growth. By focusing on understanding ourselves and our own experiences, we can approach dream interpretation with authenticity and integrity.
- **Integration and application:** The insights gained from lucid dreams should be integrated into our waking lives in a responsible and thoughtful manner. Applying dream-inspired actions should be done with consideration for ourselves and others, aligning with our values, and promoting positive transformation.

In conclusion, lucid dreaming offers a dynamic and profound connection to dream interpretation. By becoming aware of our dreams, we gain the ability to actively explore symbols, engage in real-time analysis, and integrate dream symbolism into our waking lives. Through ethical practices and a commitment to personal growth, lucid dreaming becomes a powerful tool for unlocking the depths of dream symbolism, fostering self-understanding, and navigating the intricate landscapes of the subconscious mind.

TECHNIQUES FOR LUCID DREAM INTERPRETATION

Lucid dreaming provides a unique opportunity to explore and interpret the symbolic language of dreams in a conscious and interactive manner. In this section, we delve into specific techniques that can enhance the process of lucid dream interpretation, enabling us to uncover deeper layers of meaning and gain profound insights into ourselves and our lives.

8. Dream Recall Enhancement:

Before delving into the interpretation of lucid dreams, it is essential to cultivate a strong foundation of dream recall. The following techniques can help improve your ability to remember and document your dreams with clarity and detail:

- **Dream journaling:** As discussed earlier in this chapter, keeping a dream journal is a fundamental practice for dream recall. Consistently recording your dreams immediately upon waking reinforces your dream memory and trains your mind to pay closer attention to dream experiences.

- **Mnemonic devices:** Employ memory-enhancing techniques such as mnemonic devices to aid in dream recall. For example, creating a memorable phrase or acronym based on keywords from your dream can assist in retaining and retrieving dream memories.
- **Morning routine:** Establish a morning routine that includes a few minutes of reflection on your dreams. By consciously focusing on your dreams upon waking, you signal to your mind that dreams are important and worth remembering.
- **Affirmations:** Use positive affirmations before sleep to program your mind for improved dream recall. Repeat statements such as "I remember my dreams with clarity" or "I wake up with vivid dream memories" to reinforce your intention to recall your dreams.

9. Symbolic Amplification:

Lucid dreaming allows for an in-depth exploration of dream symbols and their significance. Symbolic amplification techniques can help extract deeper meanings from dream symbolism.

- **Engage the senses:** In a lucid dream, consciously engage your senses to amplify the symbolism. Pay attention to how symbols look, feel, sound, smell, and taste. By immersing yourself fully in the sensory experience, you can unlock additional layers of symbolism and gain a more profound understanding of their meaning.
- **Symbolic questioning:** interact directly with dream symbols and ask them questions. In a lucid dream, you can engage in dialogue with symbols, asking them about their purpose, message, or personal significance. The responses you receive can provide valuable insights and facilitate interpretation.
- **Symbolic Transformations:** Experiment with transforming dream symbols to gain further understanding. In a lucid dream, intentionally change the form or nature of a symbol and observe how it evolves. This process of transformation can reveal underlying meanings and shed light on the symbol's relevance to your waking life.
- **Symbolic dialogue:** Engage in conversations with dream characters or dream figures to explore their relationship to dream symbols. Ask them about their understanding of the symbolism and their

role within the dream narrative. Their perspectives can offer new perspectives and interpretations.

10. Reflective Analysis:

Once you have engaged with dream symbols and amplified their meanings within lucid dreams, it is crucial to engage in reflective analysis. The following techniques can assist in gaining insights from your lucid dream experiences:

- **Journal reflections:** After a lucid dream, take the time to reflect on your experiences and record your thoughts and impressions in your dream journal. Write down your initial reactions, emotions, and any insights that emerged during the dream. This reflective process helps solidify the dream memory and allows for deeper analysis later on.
- **Free association:** Engage in free association exercises to explore the personal connections and associations that arise from dream symbolism. Write down the symbol and allow your mind to freely associate related ideas, memories, or emotions. This process can uncover hidden meanings and personal relevance.

- **Dream symbols inventory:** Create a dream symbols inventory by listing recurring symbols or themes that appear in your lucid dreams. Take note of their frequency, variations, and emotional impact. Over time, patterns may emerge, providing valuable clues to their significance and relevance to your life.
- **Jungian archetypes:** Utilize the framework of Carl Jung's archetypes to analyze dream symbolism. Explore how dream symbols may relate to universal archetypal patterns and the collective unconscious. This approach can offer a broader perspective on the symbolism encountered in your lucid dreams.

11. Collaborative Interpretation:

Lucid dreaming and dream interpretation can also benefit from collaborative efforts. Engaging in discussions with others who share an interest in dreams and symbolism can provide fresh insights and alternative perspectives. Consider the following collaborative techniques:

- **Dream sharing groups:** Join a dream sharing group or online community where individuals gather to discuss and interpret their dreams. Sharing your lucid dream experiences and listening to others' interpretations can broaden your understanding and offer different viewpoints.

- **Dream mentoring:** Seek out a mentor or guide experienced in dream interpretation who can provide guidance and support in understanding your lucid dreams. Their expertise and knowledge can help unravel complex symbolism and offer valuable insights.
- **Dream dialogue:** Engage in dream dialogues with trusted friends or family members. Share your lucid dreams with each other and discuss the symbolism and meanings you perceive. This collaborative exploration can spark new ideas, interpretations, and personal insights.

In conclusion, techniques for lucid dream interpretation encompass various strategies to enhance dream recall, amplify symbolism, engage in reflective analysis, and foster collaborative exploration. By incorporating these techniques into your lucid dreaming practice, you can unlock the rich tapestry of your dreams, gain profound insights, and embark on a transformative journey of self-discovery and personal growth. Remember that dream interpretation is a deeply personal and subjective process, and the true meaning of your dreams lies within your own experiences and understanding.

CONCLUSION

Dream interpretation is a powerful tool for self-discovery, personal growth, and understanding the depths of our subconscious minds. Through the practice of lucid dreaming, we can unlock the profound symbolism and messages embedded within our dreams, gaining invaluable insights into our waking lives. By utilizing techniques such as reality checks, dialogue with dream characters, symbolic exploration, and guided visualization, we can enhance our ability to interpret and understand our dreams. Dream interpretation is a lifelong journey, continually providing us with opportunities for self-reflection, healing, and spiritual growth. Embrace the mysteries of your dreams and embark on a transformative exploration of your inner world.

Part II

Techniques for Inducing and Controlling Lucid Dreams

CHAPTER 4

Reality Testing

INTRODUCTION

Welcome to Chapter 4 of our lucid dreaming journey! In this chapter, we will embark on an immersive exploration of reality testing, a foundational practice that forms the backbone of lucid dreaming. If you've ever wondered how to distinguish between the dream world and reality, or if you've yearned to unlock the key to conscious control within your dreams, then reality testing is a vital technique you need to master.

The concept of reality itself has captivated philosophers, scientists, and thinkers throughout history. From Descartes' famous statement, "Cogito, ergo sum" (I think, therefore I am), to the mind-bending musings of Plato's Allegory of the Cave, humanity has grappled with the nature of reality and its illusory qualities. Lucid dreaming, in essence, invites us to take a leap beyond the boundaries of our perceived reality and immerse ourselves in a realm where the mind transcends the limitations imposed by the physical world.

So, what exactly is reality testing, and why is it essential for lucid dreaming? Reality testing is a technique that helps us question and assess whether we are currently in a dream or a waking state. It acts as a bridge between the conscious mind and the dream world, enabling us to recognize the dream state and trigger lucidity. By incorporating reality checks into our daily lives, we develop a heightened sense of self-awareness and a habitual inclination to question the reality around us.

In our waking lives, we rely on our senses to provide us with a seemingly accurate representation of the external world. We trust what we see, hear, touch, taste, and smell as indicators of what is real. However, the dream world operates on a different set of rules, often defying logic and distorting our perception. Dreams can transport us to surreal landscapes, defy the laws of physics, and challenge the very fabric of our understanding. It is within this realm that lucid dreaming allows us to consciously navigate and explore, transforming our dreams into vivid playgrounds of possibilities.

Reality testing acts as a compass, guiding us through the labyrinthine corridors of our dreams. By incorporating specific techniques and practices into our daily routines, we begin to unravel the intricacies of our dreamscapes and develop a keen eye for distinguishing between the dream world and reality. Through consistent and deliberate reality testing, we hone our ability to recognize the subtle cues and inconsistencies that mark the dream state.

Within the realm of reality testing, there are various techniques and methods that can be employed to differentiate dreams from reality. Some popular reality checks include observing your hands, examining the behavior of clocks or text, flipping light switches, looking into mirrors, or attempting to perform gravity-defying jumps. These checks serve as triggers, reminding us to question the nature of our current experience and prompting lucidity within the dream.

But reality testing goes beyond a mere checklist of actions. It is a mindset—a state of constant curiosity and skepticism that permeates our waking lives. It beckons us to question the fabric of our reality, to challenge our assumptions, and to be present in each moment. By cultivating this mindset, we develop a deep-rooted habit of self-reflection, where we question the authenticity of our surroundings and the nature of our experiences.

In the following sections, we will delve into the various reality testing techniques and explore how to personalize them to suit your preferences and lifestyle. We will also discuss strategies for integrating reality testing seamlessly into your daily routine, ensuring that the practice becomes second nature. We will address common challenges and pitfalls that may arise, equipping you with the tools to overcome doubt and solidify your connection with the dream world.

Get ready to embark on a journey of self-discovery and wonder as we uncover the profound impact that reality testing can have on your lucid dreaming practice. By honing your ability to discern dreams from reality, you will gain greater agency within your dreamscape, enabling you to shape and direct the narrative of your dream experiences. So, let us embrace the mysteries that lie beyond the threshold of reality and, together, unlock the extraordinary power of lucid dreaming through the practice of reality testing.

THE NATURE OF REALITY

To truly grasp the significance of reality testing and its role in lucid dreaming, it is essential to delve deep into the nature of reality itself. Reality, as we perceive it, is a complex interplay of sensory experiences, thoughts, emotions, and our understanding of the world around us. It is the lens through which we interpret and navigate our waking lives, forming the foundation of our beliefs and actions.

Throughout history, philosophers, scientists, and spiritual seekers have contemplated the enigma of reality. Questions such as "What is real?" and "How can we know what is real?" have sparked profound debates and shaped our understanding of the human experience. Descartes' famous statement, "Cogito, ergo sum" (I think, therefore I am), encapsulates the notion that our ability to think and perceive our existence provides evidence of our reality.

In our waking lives, we rely on our senses to provide us with information about the external world. Our eyes capture the vibrant colors and intricate details of our surroundings; our ears receive the symphony of sounds; our skin feels the textures and temperatures; our tongues taste the flavors; and our noses detect the fragrances that envelop us. These sensory inputs construct our perception of reality, giving us a sense of presence and connection with the physical realm.

However, when we enter the realm of dreams, the rules governing reality seem to shift. Dreams possess an ethereal quality where the boundaries of time, space, and logic become malleable. In dreams, we may find ourselves in fantastical landscapes, engaging in improbable scenarios, and encountering characters and events that defy the constraints of our waking world. Dreams can be both delightful and perplexing, offering a glimpse into the depths of our subconscious mind.

Lucid dreaming bridges the gap between these two worlds—waking reality and the dream realm. It invites us to navigate the realm of dreams with conscious awareness, to explore and interact with the vivid tapestry of our imagination. By becoming lucid in a dream, we transcend the limitations imposed by our waking consciousness and tap into the limitless potential of our minds.

Reality testing serves as a crucial tool for distinguishing between the dream state and wakefulness. It enables us to question the authenticity of our current experience and challenge the boundaries of what we perceive as real. The practice of reality testing cultivates a heightened sense of self-awareness, allowing us to recognize the subtle cues and anomalies that often permeate the dream state.

In the dream world, our sensory experiences can mirror those of waking life, but they can also manifest in extraordinary ways. Colors may appear more vibrant, sounds may be amplified or distorted, and our perception of time and space may undergo dramatic shifts. By engaging in reality testing, we train ourselves to question the authenticity of our sensory experiences, to critically evaluate the consistency of our surroundings, and to uncover the telltale signs that indicate we are in a dream.

The distinction between dreams and reality may seem straightforward in theory, but it can become blurred within the realm of dreams. Dreams possess a peculiar sense of realism, where we often accept the unfolding events without question. It is during these moments that reality testing becomes invaluable, acting as a reminder to question the nature of our experience and prompting us to explore the possibility of lucidity.

As we embark on the practice of reality testing, it is important to approach it with an open mind and a sense of curiosity. By adopting an attitude of skepticism and inquiry, we create a mental framework that empowers us to challenge the boundaries of our perceived reality. With each reality check, we peel back the layers of illusion and awaken to the multidimensional nature of our existence.

In the following sections, we will explore a variety of reality testing techniques and delve into practical strategies for incorporating them into your daily life. We will also address common challenges that may arise during reality testing and provide guidance on how to overcome them. By immersing ourselves in the exploration of reality testing, we pave the way for lucid dreaming adventures and unlock the immense potential that lies within the realm of dreams.

So, let us embark on this profound journey of self-discovery and revelation. Let us venture beyond the boundaries of our perceived reality and unravel the mysteries of lucid dreaming through the practice of reality testing. By questioning the nature of our experiences, we invite the extraordinary into our lives and awaken to the boundless possibilities that await us in the realm of dreams.

UNDERSTANDING REALITY AND TESTING

To fully grasp the significance and intricacies of reality testing, it is crucial to delve into its essence and understand how it functions within the context of lucid dreaming. Reality testing is a practice that bridges the gap between the waking world and the dream realm, allowing us to discern the dream state and trigger lucidity. It involves questioning the authenticity of our current experience, challenging the boundaries of what we perceive as real, and developing a heightened sense of self-awareness.

1. Questioning the Nature of Reality

At its core, reality testing involves questioning the nature of reality itself. What is real? How do we define reality? These fundamental questions have perplexed philosophers and thinkers throughout history. Reality, as we perceive it, is a construct of our senses, thoughts, and beliefs. It is a subjective interpretation of the external world, shaped by our perceptions and experiences.

In the context of lucid dreaming, reality takes on a unique dimension. Dreams possess a captivating realism that often blurs the line between the imagined and the tangible. When we are immersed in a dream, it can feel indistinguishable from waking life, complete with sensory perceptions, emotions, and intricate narratives. Reality testing acts as a beacon of awareness within the dream state, allowing us to question the authenticity of our experiences and awaken to the realization that we are dreaming.

2. Cultivating Self-Awareness:

One of the primary objectives of reality testing is to cultivate self-awareness. Self-awareness is the ability to observe and reflect on one's own thoughts, emotions, and experiences. By incorporating reality checks into our daily lives, we develop the habit of questioning the nature of our reality, whether awake or in dreams. This constant inquiry nurtures a deep sense of self-awareness that extends into the dream state, enabling us to recognize dream signs, anomalies, and triggers for lucidity.

Through self-awareness, we become active participants in our dream experiences. We break free from the autopilot mode that often dominates our waking lives and engage with the dream world with intention and presence. Self-awareness allows us to consciously shape the narrative of our dreams, unlock creative potential, and explore the depths of our subconscious mind.

3. The Role of Reality Checks:

Reality checks are practical techniques that serve as triggers for lucidity in dreams. These checks involve performing specific actions or observations to determine whether we are in a dream or wakeful state. The goal is to establish a habit of questioning reality so that it becomes second nature, both in waking life and in dreams.

There are various reality checks that one can employ, and it's important to find the ones that resonate with you personally. Some popular reality checks include:

- Observing your hands: In dreams, hands can often appear distorted or unusual.
- Examining text or clocks: In dreams, written text and digital displays can be inconsistent or change upon re-reading.
- Flipping light switches: In dreams, the act of turning on or off lights may not produce the expected result.

- Looking into mirrors: Reflections in dreams can often be distorted or show different images.
- Attempting gravity-defying jumps In dreams, our ability to defy gravity or float can be a strong indication of the dream state.

By incorporating reality checks into your daily routine, you train your mind to question the nature of your reality. It is important to perform these checks with genuine curiosity and an open mind, rather than going through the motions mechanically. The intention behind the checks is to trigger a moment of lucidity and self-awareness, allowing you to recognize that you are in a dream.

4. Integrating Reality Testing into Daily Life:

Reality testing is not limited to specific moments or activities. It is a mindset that can be integrated seamlessly into your daily life. By infusing your waking hours with a sense of curiosity and skepticism, you cultivate a continuous awareness that can carry over into your dreams.

One way to integrate reality testing is to establish cues or reminders throughout the day. For example, you can set alarms on your phone to prompt reality checks, place sticky notes with questions like "Am I dreaming?" in visible locations, or associate reality checks with daily activities such as drinking water, opening doors, or encountering specific objects.

Consistency and intention are key when it comes to integrating reality testing into your routine. By making it a habit, you create a stronger connection between your waking and dreaming states, enhancing your ability to recognize the dream world and trigger lucidity.

5. Overcoming Challenges:

Embarking on the practice of reality testing may come with its fair share of challenges. It is common to experience doubt or skepticism, especially when reality testing does not immediately lead to lucidity. It's important to remember that lucid dreaming is a skill that develops over time with practice and persistence.

If you find yourself questioning the effectiveness of reality testing or feeling discouraged, it can be helpful to keep a dream journal. Recording your dreams regularly allows you to identify patterns, dream signs, and recurring themes. This, in turn, enhances your ability to recognize when you are in a dream and increases the effectiveness of reality testing.

Additionally, practicing mindfulness and meditation can complement your reality testing efforts. These practices cultivate a heightened state of awareness and help you develop a deeper connection with your thoughts, emotions, and sensory experiences. By integrating mindfulness into your reality testing routine, you enhance your ability to stay present and attuned to the nuances of both waking life and the dream state.

In conclusion, reality testing serves as a powerful tool in the realm of lucid dreaming. By questioning the nature of reality, cultivating self-awareness, and integrating reality checks into our daily lives, we unlock the potential to navigate and shape our dreams with conscious intention. As we continue our exploration of lucid dreaming, let us embrace the practice of reality testing, embark on a journey of self-discovery, and unlock the extraordinary realm of lucidity within our dreams.

TYPES OF REALITY CHECKS

Reality checks are practical techniques that serve as triggers for lucidity in dreams. These checks involve performing specific actions or observations to determine whether we are in a dream or wakeful state. The goal is to establish a habit of questioning reality so that it becomes second nature, both in waking life and in dreams.

Let's explore some common types of reality checks that you can incorporate into your practice:

- **Hand Awareness:** Take a moment to observe your hands closely. Look at the lines, the texture of your skin, and the shape of your fingers. In dreams, hands can often appear distorted or unusual. By regularly examining your hands throughout the day, you will train your mind to perform the same observation in dreams, triggering lucidity when you notice any abnormalities.
- **Text and Clocks:** Take a few seconds to read a piece of text, such as a sign or a sentence in a book. Then, look away and read it again. In dreams, written text and digital displays can be inconsistent or change upon re-reading. By developing the habit of double-checking texts or clocks, you create an anchor of awareness that can carry over into your dreams, helping you recognize when you are dreaming.
- **Light Switches:** Whenever you enter a room, take a moment to flick the light switch on or off. In dreams, the act of turning on or off lights may not produce the expected result. The light may not change, flicker, or behave in unusual ways. By incorporating

this reality check into your daily life, you condition your mind to question the nature of your reality, preparing you for lucidity within dreams.

- **Mirrors and Reflections:** Look into a mirror and observe your reflection closely. In dreams, reflections can often be distorted or show different images. By regularly engaging with mirrors and critically examining your reflection, you create a reality testing routine that can carry over into your dream experiences. When you notice any anomalies in the reflection, you will become aware that you are in a dream.
- **Gravity and Body Awareness:** Throughout the day, take a moment to perform simple physical tasks that involve gravity, such as jumping or pushing against a solid surface. In dreams, our ability to defy gravity or float can be a strong indication of the dream state. By incorporating gravity-defying actions into your reality checks, you build a heightened sense of body awareness and train your mind to question the laws of physics within dreams.

These are examples of reality checks that you can experiment with. It's important to choose the techniques that resonate with you personally and incorporate them consistently into your daily routine. Remember, the key is to perform these checks with genuine curiosity and an open mind, actively questioning the nature of your experiences.

CHOOSING AND PERSONALIZING REALITY CHECKS

When it comes to reality testing, one size does not fit all. Each individual has unique experiences, preferences, and tendencies, which means that the effectiveness of reality checks can vary from person to person. In this section, we will explore various factors to consider when choosing and personalizing your reality checks to maximize their impact on your lucid dreaming practice.

1. **Dream Signs and Personal Symbols:**

Dream signs are elements or events that commonly occur in your dreams. These signs can serve as cues to trigger lucidity when you encounter them in your dream state. By paying attention to the recurring themes, people, places, or activities that appear in your dreams, you can identify your own unique dream signs.

Personal symbols are objects or concepts that hold special significance to you personally. They can be specific items, animals, or abstract ideas that evoke strong emotions or memories. Incorporating personal symbols into your reality checks can increase their effectiveness by creating a deeper connection and meaning in your practice.

When choosing your reality checks, consider incorporating elements related to your dream signs and personal symbols. For example, if you frequently dream about flying, you might choose a reality check that involves testing your ability to float or defy gravity. If you have a strong affinity for cats, you could incorporate a reality check that involves interacting with a cat or noticing feline characteristics.

By aligning your reality checks with your dream signs and personal symbols, you increase the chances of triggering lucidity when these elements appear in your dreams.

2. Sensory Engagement:

Engaging your senses is a powerful way to ground yourself in the present moment and enhance your self-awareness. When choosing your reality checks, consider incorporating sensory experiences that are vivid, memorable, and easily recognizable within dreams.

Here are some sensory-based reality checks to consider:

- **Visual:** Observe your surroundings closely, paying attention to details, colors, and shapes. Look for any inconsistencies or distortions that may indicate you are in a dream.
- **Auditory:** Listen carefully to the sounds around you. Notice any unusual or dream-like qualities, such as sudden changes in volume or strange noises.
- **Tactile:** Touch and feel objects in your environment. Pay attention to the textures, temperatures, and sensations. In dreams, tactile experiences can sometimes feel different or distorted.
- **Olfactory:** Take a moment to smell your surroundings. Notice any familiar or unfamiliar scents. In dreams, smells can sometimes be exaggerated or nonexistent.
- **Gustatory:** If you have access to food or drink, savor the flavors and textures. In dreams, the taste of food or drink can be unpredictable or unusual.

By engaging multiple senses during your reality checks, you create a multi-dimensional experience that can be easily remembered and recognized within the dream state.

3. Intention and Mindfulness:

The effectiveness of reality testing is greatly influenced by your mindset and level of mindfulness during the practice. It is important to approach reality checks with intention, curiosity, and an open mind. Rather than going through the motions mechanically, engage with the process fully, truly questioning the nature of your reality.

Practice mindfulness during your reality checks by bringing your full attention to the present moment. Be fully aware of your thoughts, emotions, and sensory experiences. By cultivating mindfulness, you strengthen your overall self-awareness, making it easier to recognize the dream state and trigger lucidity.

4. Consistency and Routine:

Consistency is key when it comes to reality testing. To make reality checks an effective habit, integrate them into your daily routine. Set specific times throughout the day to perform reality checks or associate them with certain activities or cues.

Create reminders for yourself, such as by setting alarms, using sticky notes, or leveraging smartphone apps. These reminders will prompt you to question your reality and perform reality checks regularly, increasing their impact on your lucid dreaming practice.

Experiment with different reality checks and find the ones that resonate with you the most. It is essential to choose reality checks that feel natural and align with your personal preferences. If a specific reality check doesn't yield the desired results, don't be discouraged. Adapt and modify your approach until you find the techniques that work best for you.

Remember, the goal is to develop a strong habit of questioning reality, building self-awareness, and training your mind to recognize the dream state. With time, patience, and personalization, reality testing can become a powerful tool in your lucid dreaming toolkit, leading to more frequent and vivid lucid dreaming experiences.

Choosing and personalizing your reality checks is a crucial step in developing a successful lucid dreaming practice. By aligning your reality checks with your dream signs and personal symbols, engaging your senses, practicing intention and mindfulness, and establishing a consistent routine, you increase the effectiveness of your reality testing and enhance your ability to recognize the dream state.

Remember to approach reality testing with curiosity, openness, and a genuine desire to question the nature of your reality. Stay patient and adaptable as you experiment with different techniques, and be willing to adjust your approach based on your own experiences and preferences.

As you continue your journey of lucid dreaming, may your reality checks serve as the gateway to the extraordinary world of lucidity within your dreams.

INTEGRATING REALITY TESTING INTO DAILY LIFE

In Chapter 3, we explored the concept of reality testing and its significance in the practice of lucid dreaming. In this section, we will delve into the practical aspects of integrating reality testing into your daily life. By making reality checks a seamless part of your routine, you will enhance your self-awareness, increase the frequency of lucid dreaming experiences, and ultimately unlock the full potential of your dream world.

1. Mindful Reminders:

One of the keys to integrating reality testing into your daily life is to create mindful reminders that prompt you to question your reality. These reminders can be in the form of alarms, notifications on your phone, sticky notes placed strategically around your living space, or even associating reality checks with specific daily activities.

For example, you can set an alarm on your phone to go off every hour as a cue to perform a reality check. Additionally, you can place sticky notes with the question "Am I dreaming?" in places where you will frequently encounter them, such as on your bedroom mirror, computer monitor, or refrigerator door. These visual reminders will trigger your awareness and prompt you to question your reality throughout the day.

2. Anchor Reality Checks to Daily Routines:

To make reality testing a seamless part of your daily life, anchor your reality checks to activities or events that occur regularly. By associating reality checks with established routines, you create a strong connection between these checks and specific triggers, making them more likely to occur automatically.

For example, you can perform a reality check every time you walk through a doorway, before and after meals, or when you use the restroom. By tying reality checks to these routine activities, you are more likely to remember to perform them consistently, increasing their effectiveness.

3. Use environmental triggers:

Your environment can provide valuable triggers for reality testing. Look for cues or elements in your surroundings that can remind you to question your reality. These triggers can be as simple as seeing a specific color, hearing a particular sound, or encountering a specific object.

For instance, if you have a favorite color, let's say blue, you can use blue objects or the sight of the color blue as a trigger for a reality check. Whenever you see something blue, pause for a moment and question whether you are dreaming. This practice helps train your mind to perform reality checks automatically when exposed to the designated triggers.

4. Dream Journaling:

Dream journaling is an essential practice in lucid dreaming, and it can also be a powerful tool for integrating reality testing into your daily life. Keep a dream journal next to your bed and make it a habit to record your dreams as soon as you wake up. This practice not only enhances dream recall but also helps you identify recurring dream signs and themes.

As you read through your dream journal, pay attention to the patterns and elements that frequently appear in your dreams. These become valuable clues for reality testing. By recognizing your dream signs, you can choose reality checks that directly relate to these signs and increase the likelihood of triggering lucidity when they occur in your dreams.

5. Team up with a reality testing partner:

Partnering with a friend or family member who is also interested in lucid dreaming can provide additional support and accountability. Share your reality testing goals with them and encourage each other to stay consistent in practicing reality checks.

You can set up regular check-ins to discuss your progress, share dream experiences, and exchange tips and techniques. Having a partner on this journey not only adds a social aspect to your practice but also keeps you motivated and engaged in the exploration of lucid dreaming.

6. Harness Technology:

In today's digital age, technology can be a valuable ally in integrating reality testing into your daily life. There are numerous smartphone apps specifically designed to assist with lucid dreaming and reality testing. These apps often include features such as reality check reminders, dream journaling tools, and even virtual reality simulations to enhance your lucid dreaming practice.

Explore different apps and find the ones that align with your needs and preferences. Experiment with different features and functionalities to discover what works best for you. Technology can serve as a powerful tool to support and reinforce your reality testing routine.

7. Cultivate a mindful mindset:

Ultimately, the success of integrating reality testing into your daily life hinges on cultivating a mindful mindset. Approach reality checks with genuine curiosity and openness, allowing yourself to question the nature of your experiences.

Stay present and mindful throughout the day, paying attention to the details of your surroundings and engaging your senses fully. By being fully aware of your thoughts, emotions, and sensory experiences, you develop a heightened state of self-awareness that can seamlessly transition into your dream state.

Integrating reality testing into your daily life is a transformative practice that enhances self-awareness, triggers lucid dreaming experiences, and deepens your connection with the dream world. By creating mindful reminders, anchoring reality checks to daily routines, utilizing environmental triggers, journaling your dreams, partnering with others, harnessing technology, and cultivating a mindful mindset, you lay the foundation for a vibrant and fulfilling lucid dreaming practice.

Remember, consistency and intention are key. Embrace the journey of self-discovery and embrace the power of reality testing as you unlock the extraordinary potential of lucid dreaming in your life.

ENHANCING SELF-AWARENESS

In the realm of lucid dreaming, self-awareness is a fundamental skill that plays a pivotal role in achieving and maintaining lucidity within dreams. In this section, we will explore various techniques and practices that can enhance your self-awareness, leading to a deeper understanding of your thoughts, emotions, and experiences both in the waking world and the dream state.

1. Mindfulness Meditation:

Mindfulness meditation is a powerful practice that cultivates present-moment awareness and deepens your connection to the present experience. By engaging in regular mindfulness meditation sessions, you can develop a heightened sense of self-awareness that carries over into your dreams.

Set aside a dedicated time each day to practice mindfulness meditation. Find a quiet and comfortable space, close your eyes, and bring your attention to your breath. Notice the sensations of each inhalation and exhalation, and gently bring your focus back to the breath whenever your mind wanders.

As you develop your meditation practice, you will become more attuned to the fluctuations of your thoughts and emotions. This heightened awareness will extend into your dream state, making it easier to recognize the inconsistencies and peculiarities that indicate you are dreaming.

2. Reflective Journaling:

Journaling is a valuable tool for self-reflection and self-awareness. By regularly writing down your thoughts, emotions, and experiences, you can gain insight into your subconscious patterns and beliefs. Journaling can also help you identify recurring themes or symbols that appear in your dreams, providing valuable cues for reality testing.

Set aside time each day to journal about your experiences, both in the waking world and the dream realm. Reflect on your emotions, events, and interactions, and explore any connections or patterns that arise. This process of self-reflection deepens your understanding of yourself, enhances your self-awareness, and strengthens your ability to recognize the dream state.

3. Body Awareness Exercises:

Developing a strong connection with your physical body is crucial for self-awareness, as sensations and physical cues play a significant role in lucid dreaming. Engaging in body awareness exercises can heighten your sensory perception and enable you to recognize the subtle shifts and sensations within your dreams.

Practice body scans, where you systematically bring your attention to each part of your body, starting from the top of your head and moving down to your toes. Notice any areas of tension, warmth, or relaxation. By regularly engaging in body awareness exercises, you develop a greater sensitivity to the physical sensations within your dreams, making it easier to differentiate between the dream state and reality.

4. Reflecting on Daily Experiences:

Take time each day to reflect on your experiences, both significant and mundane. Cultivate a habit of introspection and ask yourself questions that encourage self-awareness. Consider the emotions you felt throughout the day, the decisions you made, and the impact they had on your overall well-being.

By consciously reflecting on your daily experiences, you develop a habit of observation and introspection that extends into your dream state. This reflective mindset enables you to question the nature of your experiences, notice inconsistencies, and trigger lucidity within your dreams.

5. Mindful Observation:

Engage in mindful observation throughout your day by consciously noticing the details of your surroundings. Take in the sights, sounds, smells, and textures of your environment. Pay attention to the subtleties that often go unnoticed in the hustle and bustle of daily life.

Practicing mindful observation sharpens your sensory awareness and strengthens your ability to notice the peculiarities and dream-like qualities within your dreams. By training yourself to be fully present and observant in your waking life, you develop the skills necessary to recognize the dream state and maintain lucidity.

6. Embodied Movement Practices:

Embodied movement practices, such as yoga, tai chi, or qigong, can significantly contribute to enhancing self-awareness. These practices emphasize the mind-body connection, allowing you to cultivate a heightened sense of awareness of your physical sensations, movements, and breath.

Engage in a regular embodied movement practice that resonates with you. As you move mindfully and attentively, focus on the sensations in your body, the rhythm of your breath, and the alignment of your posture. This intentional embodiment enhances your overall self-awareness, which extends into your dreams and supports your lucid dreaming practice.

Enhancing self-awareness is a vital component of reality testing and lucid dreaming. By incorporating practices such as mindfulness meditation, reflective journaling, body awareness exercises, reflecting on daily experiences, mindful observation, and embodied movement, you deepen your understanding of yourself and cultivate a heightened sense of awareness.

Developing self-awareness not only enriches your waking life but also enhances your ability to recognize the dream state, leading to more frequent and vivid lucid dreaming experiences. Embrace these practices with dedication and curiosity as you embark on a journey of self-discovery and lucidity within your dreams.

CHALLENGES AND PITFALLS

While reality testing is a powerful tool for lucid dreaming, it is essential to acknowledge and navigate the challenges and pitfalls that may arise during the practice. In this section, we will explore common obstacles that can hinder the effectiveness of reality testing and provide strategies to overcome them, ensuring a successful and fulfilling lucid dreaming journey.

1. **Inconsistent Practice:**

Consistency is key when it comes to reality testing. One of the primary challenges is maintaining a regular practice. It can be easy to forget or neglect reality checks, especially when life gets busy or routines change.

To overcome this challenge, establish a clear and achievable schedule for reality testing. Set reminders on your phone or use apps specifically designed for lucid dreaming to prompt you throughout the day. Make reality checks a non-negotiable part of your routine, just like brushing your teeth or eating meals.

2. **Lack of Self-Awareness:**

Some individuals struggle with cultivating self-awareness, which is crucial for effective reality testing. It can be challenging to stay present and observant amidst the distractions and demands of daily life.

To address this, incorporate mindfulness practices into your daily routine. Engage in meditation, reflective journaling, and body awareness exercises to heighten your self-awareness. By developing a mindful mindset, you will naturally become more attuned to the present moment, making reality testing a more effortless and natural process.

3. Skepticism and Doubt:

It is common to experience skepticism and doubt when practicing reality testing. You may question whether it is worth the effort or if it will truly lead to lucid dreaming experiences.

To combat skepticism, remind yourself of the countless individuals who have successfully achieved lucid dreams through reality testing. Read success stories, join online communities, and connect with fellow lucid dreamers who can share their experiences and offer support. Surrounding yourself with a positive and encouraging community can help bolster your belief in the power of reality testing.

4. Dream Amnesia:

Dream amnesia, or the inability to remember dreams upon waking, can pose a challenge when it comes to reality testing. If you can't recall your dreams, it becomes challenging to identify dream signs or triggers for reality checks.

To address dream amnesia, make dream journaling a consistent practice. Keep a dream journal by your bed and write down any fragments or snippets of dreams you can recall, even if they seem vague or incomplete. Over time, your dream recall will improve, allowing you to identify patterns and dream signs that can guide your reality testing.

5. Automatic Responses:

Another challenge is the tendency to perform reality checks mindlessly or without genuine curiosity. Sometimes, reality testing becomes a mere habit rather than an intentional practice.

To avoid automatic responses, cultivate a sense of genuine curiosity and wonder. Approach reality checks with a beginner's mind, even if you have been practicing for a long time. Cultivate a genuine interest in questioning your reality and exploring the possibilities of lucid dreaming. This mindset shift will infuse your reality testing with renewed energy and intention.

6. False Awakenings:

False awakenings, where you dream of waking up but are still within the dream, can be disorienting and undermine your reality testing efforts. You may perform reality checks within the dream, only to be deceived by the dream's convincing illusion of wakefulness.

To navigate false awakenings, incorporate reality checks into your waking routine as well. Perform a reality check immediately upon waking up, regardless of whether you think you are still dreaming or not. This practice builds a strong habit of questioning reality, increasing the chances of recognizing false awakenings and triggering lucidity within them.

7. Frustration and Impatience:

Patience is crucial in the practice of lucid dreaming. It may take time before reality testing leads to consistent lucid dream experiences. Frustration and impatience can arise when results do not come as quickly as desired.

To combat frustration and impatience, embrace the journey rather than focusing solely on the destination. View each reality testing practice as an opportunity for self-discovery and personal growth. Celebrate small victories along the way, such as increased dream recall or even fleeting moments of lucidity. By cultivating a mindset of gratitude and perseverance, you can navigate the challenges with resilience and joy.

Reality testing is a transformative practice that opens the doors to lucid dreaming. By acknowledging and addressing the challenges and pitfalls that may arise, you can ensure a more successful and fulfilling lucid dreaming journey.

Stay consistent, cultivate self-awareness, address skepticism and doubt, overcome dream amnesia, avoid automatic responses, navigate false awakenings, and practice patience and resilience. With determination and a positive mindset, you can overcome these challenges and harness the power of reality testing to unlock the extraordinary potential of lucid dreaming in your life.

CONCLUSION

Reality testing is a fundamental practice for anyone aspiring to explore the depths of lucid dreaming. By questioning the nature of reality throughout our waking lives, we develop the ability to discern the dream state from wakefulness. Through the integration of reality checks into our daily routines, we enhance our self-awareness, paving the way for lucid dreaming experiences. So, embrace the power of reality testing and open the doors to extraordinary dream adventures and self-discovery. In the next chapter, we will explore another powerful technique for inducing lucid dreams: wake-initiated lucid dreaming (WILD).

CHAPTER 5

Wake-Initiated Lucid Dreaming (WILD)

INTRODUCTION

Welcome to the extraordinary realm of wake-initiated lucid dreaming (WILD), a technique that opens the door to an exhilarating and transformative lucid dream experience. Have you ever yearned to seamlessly transition from wakefulness to the boundless landscapes of your dreams while maintaining unwavering awareness? If so, WILD is the technique that can transport you to a world where your imagination becomes tangible and your consciousness takes flight.

In this chapter, we will embark on an immersive exploration of wake-initiated lucid dreaming, unraveling its intricacies and unveiling its profound potential. We will delve into the step-by-step process, discussing the benefits and risks associated with this technique. Moreover, we will provide you with practical tips and guidance to help you enhance your WILD practice and embark on awe-inspiring journeys within your own mind.

Imagine a scenario where you find yourself effortlessly transitioning from a waking state to a vivid dream landscape, fully aware that you are dreaming. The sights, sounds, and sensations around you become vivid and malleable, responding to your every thought and desire. You can fly through star-studded skies, explore ancient civilizations, converse with dream characters, or even delve into the deepest recesses of your subconscious mind. Within the realm of lucid dreaming, the possibilities are limited only by the boundaries of your imagination.

Wake-initiated lucid dreaming offers a unique approach to lucidity—one that distinguishes itself from other techniques. Unlike methods that rely on recognizing the dream state from within a dream, WILD allows you to step directly into a lucid dream while maintaining uninterrupted consciousness. By mastering the art of maintaining awareness as you traverse the threshold between wakefulness and the dream state, you can embark on an extraordinary adventure within the expansive realm of lucid dreaming.

The concept of "wild" has fascinated and captivated lucid dreamers for ages. Throughout history, individuals have sought ways to bridge the gap between the conscious and unconscious realms, delving into the enigmatic nature of dreams. Ancient wisdom traditions, such as Tibetan Dream Yoga, have explored the profound potential of lucid dreaming and its connection to spiritual growth and self-realization. Over time, modern research and the shared experiences of countless lucid dreamers have refined and expanded our understanding of WILD.

As we embark on this journey, it is essential to approach wake-initiated lucid dreaming with an open mind, curiosity, and dedication. The path to mastering WILD may require patience and persistence. Like any skill, it is through practice and consistent effort that we unlock its full potential. While some individuals may experience success with WILD relatively quickly, others may require more time to refine their technique and cultivate the necessary skills.

Throughout this chapter, we will guide you through each stage of the WILD process, equipping you with the knowledge and tools to embark on this extraordinary adventure. We will explore the preparations necessary to create an ideal environment for WILD, the techniques to enter a hypnagogic state, and the methods to anchor your awareness as you transition into the dream world. We will also address the potential benefits and risks of WILD and provide valuable tips to maximize your chances of success.

Remember, the journey of wake-initiated lucid dreaming is as much about self-discovery and personal growth as it is about exploration and exhilaration. As you venture deeper into the realm of lucid dreaming, you may unlock hidden aspects of yourself, gain insights into your dreams, and even discover new realms of creativity and inspiration. The boundaries between reality and the dream world become blurred, allowing you to tap into the vast reservoir of untapped potential within your mind.

So, take a deep breath, let go of any doubts or preconceived notions, and open yourself to the wonders that WILD can offer. Prepare to transcend the limitations of your waking existence and embark on a journey into the depths of your consciousness. The realm of wake-initiated lucid dreaming awaits you, ready to reveal its mysteries and unleash the power of your dreams. Are you ready to step into a world where the impossible becomes possible? Let us begin.

UNDERSTANDING WAKE-INITIATED LUCID DREAMING (WILD)

Wake-initiated lucid dreaming, commonly known as WILD, is a captivating and intricate technique that holds the key to unlocking profound lucid dream experiences. In the realm of WILD, dreamers embark on an extraordinary journey that allows them to seamlessly transition from a state of wakefulness to the dream world while maintaining conscious awareness. It is a process that blurs the boundaries between reality and dreams, inviting dreamers to explore the depths of their own consciousness and tap into the limitless possibilities of the dream state.

To truly grasp the essence of WILD, it is crucial to comprehend the unique characteristics and intricacies that set it apart from other lucid dreaming techniques. Unlike methods that involve becoming aware within a dream, WILD allows dreamers to directly enter a dream without losing consciousness or awareness. This means that from the moment the dream unfolds, the dreamer is fully immersed in the dream environment, experiencing it with lucidity and clarity.

The origins of wake-initiated lucid dreaming can be traced back to ancient practices and wisdom traditions that recognized the power and significance of dreams. For instance, in Tibetan

Dream Yoga, practitioners cultivate the ability to maintain awareness during the transition from waking to dreaming, viewing dreams as a sacred and transformative space for spiritual exploration. The essence of WILD resonates with these ancient teachings, bridging the gap between the conscious and unconscious realms.

In modern times, the concept of WILD has gained increasing attention and popularity within the lucid dreaming community. Lucid dreamers from various backgrounds have contributed to refining and understanding the intricacies of this technique through personal experiences and shared insights. Their collective knowledge has illuminated the path for newcomers to embrace and explore the potential of WILD.

Central to understanding WILD is grasping the concept of the hypnagogic state—the transitional phase between wakefulness and sleep. As you embark on a WILD journey, you will encounter the fascinating interplay between wakeful awareness and the emerging dream elements. The hypnagogic state is a delicate and ephemeral space where wakefulness and dreams coexist, characterized by a tapestry of vivid sensory experiences, fleeting images, and introspective thoughts.

Entering the hypnagogic state requires a gentle surrender to the natural rhythms of the mind and body. It is a dance between relaxation and focus, where the dreamer must find the balance that allows them to maintain awareness while surrendering to the inevitable pull of sleep. Achieving this balance often requires practice, patience, and an understanding of the unique nuances that accompany the transition.

One of the fundamental elements of WILD is anchoring awareness, a technique used to prevent the dreamer from slipping into unconscious sleep during the hypnagogic state. This anchor serves as a lifeline, keeping the dreamer connected to their wakeful consciousness as they traverse the threshold into the dream world. Common anchors include a repetitive mantra, counting, or focusing on a specific sensation, such as the breath or the feeling of lying in bed. By anchoring your awareness, you create a bridge that spans the gap between wakefulness and the dream state.

Navigating the transition from the hypnagogic state to a fully realized lucid dream is a fascinating and often surreal experience. As you deepen your practice, you may find yourself encountering various sensory hallucinations—vivid visual imagery, auditory sensations, or even physical sensations that seem to emanate from within the dream environment. These manifestations are known as hypnagogic imagery or hallucinations, and they serve as signposts indicating that you are on the precipice of entering the lucid dream state.

As you venture further into the hypnagogic state, the dream world begins to unfold before you. It is a moment of sheer awe and wonder as you step into a realm shaped by your own imagination. The dreamscape becomes a vivid canvas where you have the power to shape the environment, interact with dream characters, and explore the depths of your subconscious mind.

However, it is important to note that the journey to mastering WILD requires patience, dedication, and practice. While some individuals may experience success with WILD relatively quickly, others may require more time to refine their technique and develop the necessary skills. Each person's experience with WILD is unique, and it is essential to approach the practice with an open mind and a willingness to embrace the learning process.

In the next sections of this chapter, we will explore the step-by-step process of wake-initiated lucid dreaming in greater detail. We will delve into the preparations necessary to create an optimal environment for WILD practice, the techniques to enter the hypnagogic state, and the methods to anchor your awareness during the transition into the dream world. Additionally, we will discuss the potential benefits and risks associated with WILD and provide valuable tips to enhance your WILD practice.

Remember, wake-initiated lucid dreaming is not just a tool for entertainment or escapism; it is a gateway to profound self-discovery, personal growth, and expanded consciousness. By venturing into the depths of your own mind, you may uncover hidden aspects of yourself, gain insights into your dreams, and tap into boundless creativity and inspiration.

So, let us embark on this incredible journey together. Prepare to unravel the mysteries of wake-initiated lucid dreaming and step into a world where dreams become tangible realities. The realm of WILD awaits, ready to unlock the extraordinary potential of your dreams. Are you ready to take the first step into the infinite expanses of your own consciousness? Let us begin.

THE WILD PROCESS

The wake-initiated lucid dreaming (WILD) process is a multifaceted and intricate journey that requires a delicate balance of relaxation, focus, and self-awareness. It involves traversing the threshold between wakefulness and the dream state while maintaining consciousness and intention. By understanding the various stages and techniques involved in the WILD process, you can enhance your chances of successfully experiencing lucid dreams. In this section, we will explore the step-by-step process of WILD in detail, providing valuable insights and practical guidance to help you navigate this extraordinary realm.

1. Preparation:

Before delving into the WILD process, it is essential to create an optimal environment that promotes relaxation and enhances your ability to enter the hypnagogic state. Consider the following factors:

- **Sleep Schedule:** Establish a consistent sleep schedule that allows for an adequate amount of sleep each night. Consistency in sleep patterns helps regulate your body's internal clock and improves your overall sleep quality.
- **Sleep Hygiene:** Adopt healthy sleep hygiene practices, such as avoiding caffeine and stimulating activities close to bedtime, maintaining a comfortable sleep environment, and engaging in relaxation techniques before sleep.
- **Intention Setting:** Set a clear intention to have a lucid dream through WILD. This intention will serve as a focal point and reinforce your commitment to achieving lucidity during the dream state.

- **Dream Journaling:** Maintain a dream journal and develop the habit of recording your dreams upon waking. This practice will enhance your dream recall and help you identify dream signs and patterns, which can increase your chances of recognizing when you are dreaming during the WILD process.

2. Relaxation:

The first step in the WILD process is achieving a state of deep relaxation. This allows your mind and body to enter a calm and receptive state, making it easier to transition into the hypnagogic state. Consider the following relaxation techniques:

- **Progressive Muscle Relaxation:** Start by tensing and then relaxing each muscle group in your body, progressing from your toes to your head. This technique promotes physical relaxation and releases tension.
- **Deep Breathing:** Engage in slow, deep breathing exercises to calm your mind and promote relaxation. Focus on the sensation of your breath as you inhale and exhale, allowing yourself to enter a state of deep relaxation with each breath.

- **Meditation:** Practice meditation techniques, such as mindfulness meditation or guided visualizations, to quiet your mind, cultivate present-moment awareness, and enhance your ability to maintain focus during the WILD process.

3. **Entry into the Hypnagogic State:**

As relaxation deepens, you will enter the hypnagogic state—the transitional phase between wakefulness and sleep. This is a crucial stage in the WILD process, as it sets the foundation for entering the lucid dream state. Here are some techniques to facilitate entry into the hypnagogic state:

- **Visualization:** Close your eyes and visualize a peaceful and serene scene, such as a calm beach or a tranquil forest. Engage your senses and imagine the sights, sounds, and even textures of this imagined environment, immersing yourself in the experience.
- **Mental Affirmations:** Repeat positive affirmations or mantras silently in your mind. Examples include phrases like "I am aware and present in my dreams" or "I will lucid dream tonight." This practice helps

reinforce your intention to have a lucid dream and enhances your mental focus.

- **Hypnagogic Imagery:** As you enter the hypnagogic state, you may experience various sensory hallucinations, including vivid visual images or auditory sensations. Embrace these experiences and allow them to guide you deeper into the dream state.

4. Anchoring Awareness:

Anchoring awareness is a crucial step in maintaining consciousness during the transition from the hypnagogic state to the dream state. By anchoring your awareness, you ensure that you remain cognizant and present as you enter a lucid dream. Consider the following techniques:

- **Mantra Repetition:** Choose a simple word or phrase, such as "I am lucid" or "I am dreaming," and repeat it mentally or verbally. The rhythmic repetition of the mantra helps anchor your awareness and prevent you from drifting into unconsciousness.
- **Sensory Focus:** Direct your attention to a specific sensation, such as the feeling of your breath or the weight of your body on the bed. By focusing on this sensation, you

maintain a connection to your physical body while transitioning into the dream state.

- **Visualizations:** Visualize yourself within the dream environment, actively engaging with the surroundings, and maintaining a clear image of your desired dream scenario. By vividly picturing yourself in the dream, you anchor your awareness to the upcoming lucid experience.

5. **Entering the Lucid Dream:**

As you progress through the WILD process and anchor your awareness, you will reach the threshold where the dream state fully emerges. The transition into a lucid dream can vary in intensity and duration for each individual. Here are some pointers to facilitate a smooth entry into a lucid dream:

- **Retain Awareness:** As you feel the dream state enveloping you, maintain your awareness and clarity of thought. Remind yourself that you are dreaming and that you have entered the lucid dream state. By holding onto your awareness, you can fully engage with the dream environment.
- **Stabilization Techniques:** Once you are fully immersed in the lucid dream, it is

helpful to stabilize the dream environment. Rub your hands together, spin in circles, or engage your senses by touching and observing the dream world around you. These actions help solidify your presence in the dream and prolong the lucid experience.

- **Intention Manifestation:** With lucidity firmly established, you can now direct your attention towards manifesting specific intentions within the dream. This can include exploring dream landscapes, interacting with dream characters, or embarking on personal quests for self-discovery and growth.

6. Dream Control and Exploration:

Once you have successfully entered the lucid dream state, the possibilities are limitless. You have the power to shape and manipulate the dream environment according to your desires. Experiment with various techniques to exert control over the dream, such as:

- **Telekinesis:** Use your mind to move objects within the dream world, testing the boundaries of your control and expanding your understanding of dream physics.

- **Flying:** Embrace the exhilaration of flight, soaring through the dreamy skies with freedom and joy. Feel the wind on your face and revel in the sense of liberation.
- **Conversations with Dream Characters:** Engage in dialogue with the dream characters you encounter. Ask them questions, seek guidance, or engage in deep conversations that provide insights into your subconscious mind.
- **Exploring Dream Landscapes:** Venture into unexplored dream landscapes, unveiling hidden realms, and encountering breathtaking sights. Embrace the adventure and allow your curiosity to guide you through the dream world.

7. Dream Recall and Integration:

After awakening from a lucid dream, it is essential to document your experiences in your dream journal. Take note of the details, emotions, and insights gained during the dream state. Reflect on the significance of the dream and consider how it may relate to your waking life. This process of dream recall and integration strengthens the connection between your conscious and subconscious minds, allowing for further self-discovery and personal growth.

As you continue your journey with WILD, remember that each attempt is an opportunity for growth and exploration. Be patient and persistent, and embrace the learning process. With time and practice, the boundaries of your dreams will expand, and the depth of your lucid experiences will deepen.

In the next section, we will explore the benefits and potential risks of WILD, providing you with a comprehensive understanding of the practice. Let us continue to unravel the power of wake-initiated lucid dreaming and embark on a transformative journey of self-discovery and exploration.

BENEFITS AND RISKS OF WILD

Wake-initiated lucid dreaming (WILD) is a fascinating practice that offers a multitude of benefits, ranging from personal growth and self-discovery to enhanced creativity and problem-solving. However, like any practice involving altered states of consciousness, it is essential to be aware of potential risks and challenges. In this section, we will explore the benefits and risks of WILD in detail, providing you with a comprehensive understanding of what to expect as you embark on your journey of wake-initiated lucid dreaming.

BENEFITS OF WILD:

- **Lucid Dream Control:** One of the primary benefits of WILD is the ability to have complete control and agency within the dream world. As you become proficient in WILD, you can actively shape the dream environment, interact with dream characters, and explore your subconscious mind with intention. This level of control allows for unparalleled experiences of self-expression and creativity.
- **Personal Growth and Self-Discovery:** Lucid dreaming through WILD can serve as a powerful tool for personal growth and self-exploration. By consciously navigating your dreams, you can delve into your subconscious mind, confront fears, uncover hidden desires, and gain valuable insights into your emotions, beliefs, and motivations. This self-awareness can lead to personal transformation and a deeper understanding of oneself.
- **Emotional Healing:** WILD provides an opportunity to engage with unresolved emotional issues and facilitate healing. Within the lucid dream state, you can confront and process challenging emotions, traumas, and anxieties in a safe and controlled environment. By working

through these experiences, you may find emotional release, catharsis, and a renewed sense of emotional well-being.

- **Enhanced Creativity:** Lucid dreaming has been known to enhance creativity and innovation. By tapping into the boundless imagination of the dream world, you can generate new ideas, explore artistic expressions, and find inspiration for creative projects. Many artists, writers, and musicians have credited lucid dreaming with providing them with fresh perspectives and breakthrough moments of creative insight.
- **Problem-Solving and Decision Making:** WILD can be a valuable tool for problem-solving and decision-making. Within the lucid dream state, you can explore different scenarios, test hypotheses, and experiment with potential solutions to real-life challenges. This creative problem-solving approach can provide unique perspectives and help you make informed decisions in your daily life.

Transcendent Experiences: Wake-initiated lucid dreaming has the potential to offer profound transcendent experiences. Some individuals report spiritual encounters, out-of-body experiences, and a sense of interconnectedness with the universe during their lucid dream journeys. These experiences can be deeply transformative, fostering a greater sense of purpose, meaning, and spiritual connection.

RISKS AND CHALLENGES OF WILD:

- **Sleep Disruptions:** Engaging in WILD requires a level of wakefulness during the sleep process, which can lead to sleep disruptions. It may take time and practice to find a balance between wakefulness and relaxation, and some individuals may experience difficulty falling asleep or maintaining sleep during their WILD attempts. It is important to prioritize overall sleep hygiene and ensure an adequate amount of restful sleep.
- **Sleep Paralysis:** During the transition from wakefulness to the dream state in WILD, some individuals may experience episodes of sleep paralysis. A brief inability to move or speak, often accompanied by vivid hallucinations, is sleep paralysis. While these experiences can be unsettling, understanding their nature and remaining calm can help alleviate any anxiety associated with sleep paralysis.

- **Dream Intensity:** Lucid dreams can be exceptionally vivid and emotionally intense. For individuals who are sensitive to intense emotions or prone to nightmares, the heightened reality of lucid dreams may be overwhelming. It is crucial to practice self-care and emotional regulation techniques to navigate the intensity of dream experiences.
- **Confusion between Dream and Reality:** Lucid dreams can blur the boundaries between the dream world and waking reality. In some instances, individuals may experience difficulty differentiating between the two, leading to confusion or disorientation upon awakening. Developing self-awareness and regularly testing reality can help maintain clarity and prevent potential confusion.
- **Time Commitment and Patience:** WILD requires dedication, patience, and persistence. Achieving lucidity through WILD can take time and practice, and it may not yield immediate results. It is essential to approach the practice with a long-term perspective, embracing the learning process and understanding that each attempt contributes to your overall progress.

- **Sleep Quality:** Engaging in WILD practices during the night may impact the overall quality of your sleep. It is important to strike a balance between exploring lucid dreaming and ensuring sufficient restful sleep. Monitoring your sleep patterns and adjusting your practice accordingly can help you maintain healthy sleep habits.

It is crucial to approach wake-initiated lucid dreaming with a balanced perspective, considering both the benefits and risks involved. By understanding the potential challenges and implementing appropriate techniques and self-care practices, you can maximize the benefits of WILD while minimizing any potential risks.

In the next chapter, we will explore another technique for lucid dreaming: mnemonic-induced lucid dreaming (MILD). This technique offers an alternative approach to achieving lucidity and can be a valuable addition to your lucid dreaming toolbox. Let us delve into the fascinating world of MILD and discover its potential for lucid dream exploration and self-discovery.

TIPS FOR SUCCESSFUL WILD PRACTICE

Wake-initiated lucid dreaming (WILD) is a technique that requires focus, patience, and a deep understanding of the transition from wakefulness to the dream state. While it may take time to master, with consistent practice and the implementation of effective strategies, you can enhance your chances of successfully inducing lucid dreams through WILD. In this section, we will explore a comprehensive list of tips and techniques to support your WILD practice and increase your likelihood of experiencing vivid and conscious dreams.

- **Establish a Consistent Sleep Routine:** Maintaining a regular sleep schedule is essential for optimizing your WILD practice. Aim to go to bed and wake up at the same time each day to regulate your sleep patterns. This consistency helps condition your mind and body for successful lucid dreaming.
- **Prioritize relaxation and sleep hygiene.** Create a sleep-friendly environment that promotes relaxation and restful sleep. Ensure your bedroom is dark, quiet, and at a comfortable temperature. Limit exposure to electronic devices before bedtime, as

the blue light emitted can interfere with melatonin production and disrupt your sleep.

- **Practice relaxation techniques.** Cultivate a state of relaxation before attempting WILD. Deep breathing exercises, progressive muscle relaxation, or mindfulness meditation can help calm your mind and body, preparing you for a focused and receptive state conducive to lucid dreaming.
- **Keep a Dream Journal:** Maintaining a dream journal is crucial for developing dream recall and increasing your dream awareness. Keep a notebook and pen by your bedside and record your dreams as soon as you wake up. Pay attention to recurring themes, symbols, and patterns, as these can serve as dream signs that trigger lucidity.
- **Perform Reality Checks:** Consistently practicing reality checks throughout the day helps train your mind to question your waking reality, increasing the chances of performing similar checks within your dreams. Common reality checks include attempting to push your finger through your palm or checking the time on a clock twice to see if it remains consistent.

- **Visualize Your Lucid Dream Goals:** Before bed, spend a few moments visualizing yourself becoming lucid in a dream and successfully engaging with your desired dream goals. Create vivid mental imagery and evoke the emotions associated with lucidity. This practice helps program your subconscious mind and sets clear intentions for your dream experiences.
- **Experiment with Sleep Positions:** Some individuals find that certain sleep positions enhance their chances of entering the lucid dream state. Experiment with lying on your back, stomach, or side to determine which position works best for you. Find a position that balances relaxation and alertness.
- **Set Alarms for the Wake-Up-and-Go (WBTB) Technique:** Incorporate the Wake-Up-and-Go (WBTB) technique into your WILD practice. Set an alarm to wake yourself up after several hours of sleep, and use this opportunity to engage in reality checks, review your dream journal, and visualize lucid dreaming. This technique takes advantage of the natural tendency to enter REM sleep more quickly after waking up.
- **Utilize Induction Aids:** Explore the use of induction aids to enhance your WILD

practice. These can include binaural beats, white noise, or ambient sounds that promote relaxation and facilitate the transition into the dream state. Experiment with different audio tracks or apps specifically designed for lucid dream induction.

- **Maintain a Gentle Focus:** As you progress through the WILD process, maintain a gentle focus on your chosen anchor point, whether it's your breath, a mantra, or a visualized scenario. Avoid becoming too intense or desperate for results, as this can interfere with relaxation and hinder the transition into the dream state.
- **Experiment with Time of Day:** While WILD attempts are typically done during the night, some individuals find success with daytime napping. Explore different times of day to practice WILD and determine when you are most receptive to the transition from wakefulness to the dream state.
- **Practice Dream Exit Techniques:** When you find yourself in a state of sleep paralysis or in a hypnagogic state during WILD, practice dream exit techniques such as rolling out of your body or visualizing yourself stepping into the dream environment. These techniques can

help facilitate a smooth transition into the lucid dream state.

- **Maintain a Positive Attitude:** Approach your WILD practice with a positive and optimistic mindset. Cultivate an attitude of curiosity, excitement, and gratitude for the journey of lucid dreaming. Celebrate small successes and view any setbacks as learning opportunities rather than failures.
- **Seek Community Support:** Engage with online forums, social media groups, or local lucid dreaming communities to connect with others who share your passion for lucid dreaming. Sharing experiences, exchanging tips, and receiving support from like-minded individuals can be inspiring and motivating for your WILD practice.
- **Be patient and persistent.** WILD is a skill that develops over time, and success may not come immediately. Be patient with yourself and trust the process. Persistently practice the techniques, maintain a consistent routine, and adapt your approach as needed. Each experience, whether lucid or not, contributes to your overall progress.

By incorporating these tips and techniques into your WILD practice, you can optimize your chances of experiencing lucid dreams and embarking on transformative journeys within the realm of consciousness. Stay committed, embrace the learning process, and prepare yourself for remarkable adventures within the lucid dream world.

In the next chapter, we will explore another popular technique for inducing lucid dreams: mnemonic-induced lucid dreaming (MILD). This technique focuses on increasing your overall dream awareness and cultivating a conscious mindset throughout your dreams. Let us dive into the realm of MILD and discover its potential for enhancing your lucid dreaming practice.

Wake-initiated lucid dreaming offers a fascinating and immersive approach to lucid dream exploration. By mastering the art of maintaining awareness as you transition into the dream state, you can unlock profound experiences and gain greater control over your dreams. Remember to approach WILD with patience, consistency, and an open mind. With practice, you will embark on remarkable adventures within the boundless realm of lucid dreaming. Now, it is time to step into your dreams and discover the limitless possibilities that await you.

Sweet dreams!

CHAPTER 6

Mnemonic-Induced Lucid Dreaming (MILD)

INTRODUCTION

Welcome to Chapter 6 of our lucid dreaming journey! Prepare to embark on an exciting exploration of the remarkable technique known as Mnemonic-Induced Lucid Dreaming (MILD). If you've ever yearned for a reliable and effective method to induce lucid dreams, MILD is poised to be a game-changer in your dream exploration endeavors.

Developed by the renowned lucid dreaming expert Stephen LaBerge, MILD combines intention setting, visualization, and mnemonic cues to enhance your chances of becoming aware and in control within the enigmatic realm of dreams.

Imagine this scenario: You find yourself wandering through a breathtaking landscape, surrounded by vibrant colors and magical creatures. Suddenly, a realization dawns upon you — you are dreaming!

With a surge of excitement, you take control, soaring through the skies, exploring uncharted territories, and engaging in exhilarating adventures that surpass the boundaries of your waking reality. Lucid dreaming offers a gateway to this extraordinary world, where your imagination knows no bounds and the impossible becomes possible. MILD is a technique that can pave the way to these exhilarating experiences, allowing you to unlock the full potential of your lucid dreaming abilities.

But what exactly is MILD, and how does it work? In this chapter, we will delve deep into the intricacies of this powerful technique, equipping you with the knowledge and tools to harness its potential. MILD is rooted in the concept of prospective memory, which involves remembering to do something in the future. In the context of lucid dreaming, MILD harnesses the power of intention setting and mnemonic cues to reinforce the awareness of being in a dream while you are dreaming. By skillfully integrating these components, MILD empowers you to recognize and seize the moments of lucidity that arise within the realm of dreams.

Before we embark on this exciting journey, it's essential to lay a strong foundation for the practice of MILD. We encourage you to take a moment to reflect on your motivations and aspirations for lucid dreaming. What draws you to this remarkable realm of consciousness? Is it the thirst for adventure, the desire for self-discovery, or the yearning to explore the uncharted territories of your subconscious mind? Understanding your personal goals and intentions will infuse your practice of MILD with purpose and passion.

Throughout this book, we have emphasized the importance of maintaining a dream journal, practicing reality testing, and cultivating self-awareness. These foundational practices serve as the pillars upon which MILD builds its framework. By consistently recording your dreams in a journal, you not only enhance your dream recall but also develop a keen observational eye for the subtle patterns and themes that emerge within your dreams. Engaging in reality testing throughout your waking hours helps cultivate a habit of questioning your reality, which can seamlessly extend into the dream world. These practices set the stage for the powerful technique of

MILD, amplifying its effectiveness and maximizing your potential for lucid dream exploration.

In the following sections of this chapter, we will guide you through the intricate steps of MILD, unveiling its inner workings and providing practical strategies for its implementation. We will explore the art of setting intentions, the significance of visualization, and the integration of mnemonic cues to heighten your lucidity within dreams. Additionally, we will address the potential benefits and risks associated with the practice of MILD, equipping you with the knowledge and awareness needed to navigate your lucid dreaming journey safely and responsibly.

As you delve into the depths of MILD, remember to approach the practice with an open mind and a sense of curiosity. Lucid dreaming is a deeply personal and transformative experience, and each individual's journey is unique. Embrace the process, celebrate each milestone, and remain patient and persistent as you cultivate the art of mnemonic-induced lucid dreaming. Are you ready to take the plunge? Let's dive in and unlock the hidden realms of lucidity that await within your dreams!

UNDERSTANDING MILD

Mnemonic-Induced Lucid Dreaming (MILD) is a fascinating technique that can significantly enhance your ability to have lucid dreams. Developed by the renowned lucid dreaming expert Stephen LaBerge, MILD combines the power of intention setting, visualization, and mnemonic cues to increase your chances of becoming aware and in control within the dream world. By understanding the intricacies of MILD and implementing its principles, you can unlock the potential of lucid dreaming and embark on awe-inspiring adventures within the realms of your own mind.

1. Setting the Foundation

Before delving into the specific steps of MILD, it's crucial to establish a strong foundation for the technique. This foundation includes three essential components: maintaining a dream journal, practicing reality testing, and cultivating self-awareness.

Keeping a dream journal is a fundamental practice in the world of lucid dreaming. By consistently recording your dreams immediately upon awakening, you strengthen your dream recall abilities. This practice creates the habit of paying closer attention to your dreams and encourages a deeper connection with your dream experiences. Additionally, maintaining a dream journal allows you to identify recurring dream themes, symbols, and patterns, which can serve as potential triggers for lucidity.

Reality testing is another vital aspect of preparing for MILD. Throughout your waking hours, make it a habit to question your reality and perform reality checks. Reality checks involve simple actions that help you determine whether you are dreaming or awake. Examples of reality checks include looking at your hands and checking if they appear normal or counting your fingers. By consistently practicing reality testing, you condition your mind to question the nature of reality, which can carry over into your dream state, triggering lucidity.

Cultivating self-awareness is the third pillar of the MILD foundation. Self-awareness involves being present and mindful throughout your daily life. By cultivating mindfulness, you develop a heightened sense of awareness, which can extend into your dreams. Paying attention to your thoughts, emotions, and sensory experiences in waking life will train your mind to notice inconsistencies or anomalies within your dreams, increasing the likelihood of becoming lucid.

2. Recall and Reflection:

The first step in the MILD technique involves improving dream recall and reflecting upon your dreams. As mentioned earlier, keeping a dream journal is instrumental in enhancing your dream recall abilities. Upon waking from a dream, take a few moments to lie still and mentally recapitulate the dream in as much detail as possible. Then, grab your dream journal and record the dream, capturing the vivid imagery, emotions, and any notable events. By consistently practicing dream recall and reflection, you strengthen the connection between your conscious and subconscious minds, paving the way for lucid dream experiences.

Reflecting on your dreams goes beyond mere documentation. It involves identifying recurring dream themes, symbols, or patterns that frequently appear in your dreams. These elements are known as dream signs. Dream signs can be people, places, objects, or events that stand out as unique or unusual. By recognizing your personal dream signs, you can use them as triggers for lucidity. For example, if you often dream of flying or encountering mythical creatures, these recurring motifs can serve as potent cues to trigger lucidity when they arise in your dreams.

3. Identifying Dream Signs:

Dream signs play a vital role in MILD and serve as cues for triggering lucidity. The identification of dream signs is a deeply personal process that requires self-reflection and attention to detail. Take some time to review your dream journal entries and identify any recurring elements or patterns. These could be specific locations, people, objects, or even emotional states that frequently appear in your dreams. Once you have identified your personal dream signs, you can use them as triggers to initiate lucidity.

4. Setting Intentions:

Intention setting is a powerful aspect of MILD. Before drifting off to sleep, clearly and consciously set your intention to become lucid in your dreams. Repeat affirmations or mantras such as, "Tonight, I will realize I am dreaming" or "I am aware and in control within my dreams." As you repeat these intentions, evoke a strong sense of belief and conviction. Visualize yourself recognizing a dream sign or becoming aware that you are dreaming and experiencing the exhilaration of lucidity. By setting clear intentions and cultivating a strong belief in your ability to become lucid, you create a powerful mindset that primes your subconscious mind for the possibility of lucid dreaming.

5. Mnemonic Cues:

Mnemonic cues are an integral part of the MILD technique. They act as mental reminders or triggers to recognize your dream signs and initiate lucidity within your dreams. Mnemonic cues can take various forms, such as visualizations, verbal cues, or mental associations. The key is to create a link between the cue and the desired outcome of becoming lucid.

One effective approach is to visualize yourself recognizing a dream sign and becoming lucid. Imagine the moment of realization, the surge of awareness, and the subsequent control you exercise within the dream. Visualize this scenario vividly, engaging your senses and emotions to make it as real and tangible as possible. By repeatedly visualizing this scenario, you reinforce the connection between the cue and the desired outcome, increasing the likelihood of experiencing lucidity.

Verbal cues can also be employed as mnemonic reminders. Before falling asleep, repeat a specific phrase or keyword associated with lucidity, such as "awareness," "lucidity," or "I am dreaming." By using these cues, you create a mental anchor that can help trigger the recognition of dream signs during your dream experiences.

Another approach is to create mental associations between your desired outcome of lucidity and specific dream signs. For example, if you frequently dream of encountering a red rose, you can mentally associate the red rose with the idea of becoming lucid. Practice mentally linking the image of the red rose with the intention to become aware in your dreams. When you encounter the red rose in a dream, the association will serve as a mnemonic trigger, reminding you to question your reality and initiate lucidity.

6. Combining Mnemonic Cues and Reality Testing:

To amplify the effectiveness of MILD, combine your mnemonic cues with reality testing. Throughout the day, continue to perform reality checks and question your reality. By consistently engaging in reality testing, you develop the habit of questioning whether you are dreaming or awake. This habit naturally extends into your dream state, increasing your chances of recognizing dream signs and triggering lucidity.

When you encounter a potential dream sign during your waking hours, perform a reality check and question whether you are dreaming. As you conduct the reality check, mentally evoke your mnemonic cues associated with lucidity. This combination of reality testing and mnemonic cues strengthens the connection between waking reality and the dream world, enhancing your chances of becoming lucid in your dreams.

7. Wake-Back-to-Bed Technique:

To further optimize the practice of MILD, you can combine it with the Wake-Back-to-Bed (WBTB) technique. Set an alarm to wake you up after approximately 4-6 hours of sleep. During this brief wakeful period, engage in activities that stimulate your mind, such as reading about lucid dreaming or reviewing your dream journal. This period of wakefulness increases your brain's alertness while preparing it for the MILD technique during the subsequent sleep period.

8. Returning to Sleep with Intention

After spending time awake, go back to bed with a clear intention to engage in MILD. Repeat your affirmations, visualize your desired outcomes, and evoke the mnemonic cues associated with lucidity. As you drift off to sleep, maintain a relaxed and receptive state of mind, allowing your intentions to permeate your subconscious. By returning to sleep with a focused intention, you create the ideal conditions for MILD to unfold.

9. Practicing Persistence and Patience:

MILD, like any skill, requires practice, persistence, and patience. It may take time to experience consistent lucid dreams using this technique. Be gentle with yourself, and celebrate even the smallest successes along the way. Each step forward is a step closer to unlocking the full potential of your lucid dreaming abilities. With consistent practice and a positive mindset, MILD can become a reliable tool in your lucid dreaming repertoire.

Understanding the intricacies of mnemonic-induced lucid dreaming (MILD) empowers you to take control of your dream experiences and explore the vast realms of lucidity within your mind. By setting a strong foundation, identifying dream signs, setting clear intentions, and utilizing mnemonic cues, you enhance your chances of becoming aware and in control of your dreams. MILD is a versatile technique that can be combined with other practices such as reality testing and the Wake-Back-to-Bed technique to amplify its effectiveness.

Remember, lucid dreaming is a deeply personal and transformative journey. Embrace the process, stay committed to your practice, and approach each experience with curiosity and wonder. With MILD as your guide, prepare to embark on extraordinary adventures within the realm of lucidity, where your dreams become a canvas for exploration, self-discovery, and limitless possibilities.

BENEFITS AND RISKS OF MILD

Mnemonic-Induced Lucid Dreaming (MILD) is a powerful technique that offers numerous benefits for those seeking to explore the world of lucid dreaming. However, like any practice, it's important to be aware of potential risks and approach MILD with caution. In this section, we will explore the benefits and risks associated with MILD, empowering you to navigate your lucid dreaming journey safely and responsibly.

BENEFITS OF MILD:

- **Increased Lucid Dream Frequency:** One of the primary benefits of MILD is its potential to increase the frequency of lucid dreams. By consistently practicing MILD and setting clear intentions, you are more likely to become aware within your dreams. This heightened frequency of lucid dreaming allows for greater exploration of the dream world and the opportunity to engage in controlled and immersive experiences.
- **Enhanced Dream Recall:** MILD encourages the development of strong dream recall skills. By maintaining a dream journal and reflecting on your dreams, you create a habit of paying closer attention to your dream experiences. This heightened awareness leads to improved dream recall, allowing you to remember and analyze your dreams in greater detail. Enhanced dream recall not only enriches your lucid dreaming practice but also provides valuable insights into your subconscious mind.

- **Personal Growth and Self-Discovery:** Lucid dreaming, facilitated by MILD, can be a profound tool for personal growth and self-discovery. Within lucid dreams, you have the opportunity to explore your innermost thoughts, emotions, and desires. You can confront fears, overcome obstacles, and gain valuable insights into your waking life. MILD provides a pathway for deep introspection, allowing you to uncover hidden aspects of yourself and facilitate personal transformation.
- **Creative Exploration:** Lucid dreaming, combined with MILD, offers a unique platform for creative exploration. Within lucid dreams, you can unleash your imagination, engage in artistic endeavors, and explore new ideas and concepts. MILD enhances your ability to consciously shape and control the dream environment, enabling you to engage in creative activities such as painting, composing music, or engaging in imaginative storytelling. The creative potential of lucid dreaming through MILD is virtually limitless.
- **Overcoming Nightmares:** MILD can be a valuable tool for overcoming nightmares and recurring distressing dreams. By becoming aware within a nightmare, you

can shift the narrative, confront your fears, and transform the dream into a positive or neutral experience. MILD equips you with the ability to take control, face your fears, and reshape the dream landscape, empowering you to overcome nightmares and find resolution within your dream world.

RISKS OF MILD:

- **Sleep Disruption:** Engaging in MILD, particularly when combined with techniques like the Wake-Back-to-Bed (WBTB) method, can disrupt your sleep patterns. Waking up during the night for the WBTB technique can result in sleep fragmentation, leading to daytime sleepiness or fatigue. It's essential to find a balance that allows for sufficient sleep while incorporating MILD into your practice.
- **False Awakenings:** False awakenings, where you dream of waking up but are still within the dream state, can occur when practicing MILD. This can lead to confusion and potentially hinder your ability to recognize the dream state. It's important to develop a strong sense of

reality testing and self-awareness to avoid being caught in a cycle of false awakenings.

- **Sleep Paralysis:** In some cases, engaging in lucid dreaming techniques like MILD can lead to episodes of sleep paralysis. Sleep paralysis occurs when the mind becomes conscious while the body remains in a state of temporary paralysis that normally accompanies REM sleep. This experience can be unsettling or frightening for some individuals. If you encounter sleep paralysis, it's important to remain calm and remind yourself that it is a temporary state that will pass.
- **Emotional Intensity:** Lucid dreams can evoke intense emotions, both positive and negative. While this emotional intensity can be a valuable aspect of the lucid dreaming experience, it's important to be prepared for the potential impact it may have on your emotions upon waking. It's advisable to approach lucid dreaming with a stable emotional state and be prepared to process and integrate the emotions that arise during your dream experiences.
- **Time Commitment and Practice:** MILD requires consistent practice and dedication to yield significant results. Developing the skills necessary for lucid dreaming

takes time and effort. It's important to set realistic expectations and understand that it may take weeks or even months to experience consistent lucidity through MILD. Patience and persistence are key.

Mnemonic-Induced Lucid Dreaming (MILD) offers a wide range of benefits for those seeking to explore the fascinating world of lucid dreaming. By practicing MILD, you can increase the frequency of lucid dreams, enhance dream recall, experience personal growth and self-discovery, engage in creative exploration, and overcome nightmares. However, it's crucial to be aware of potential risks such as sleep disruption, false awakenings, sleep paralysis, emotional intensity, and the time commitment required for consistent results.

Approach MILD with a sense of responsibility, ensuring that you prioritize your overall well-being and sleep hygiene. Stay attuned to your personal limits and adjust your practice accordingly. With proper understanding, mindfulness, and a balanced approach, MILD can be a transformative and empowering technique that opens the doors to the rich and captivating world of lucid dreaming.

Congratulations on completing Chapter 6 and gaining a comprehensive understanding of mnemonic-induced lucid dreaming (MILD). With this powerful technique in your lucid dreaming toolkit, you have the potential to unlock a world of wonder and self-discovery within your dreams. Remember to be patient, persistent, and open to the experiences that await you. In the next chapter, we will explore other techniques for inducing lucid dreams, expanding your repertoire, and increasing your chances of lucid dream success. Sweet dreams!

CHAPTER 7

Other Techniques for Lucid Dreaming

INTRODUCTION

Welcome to Chapter 7 of our lucid dreaming book, where we will dive into the exploration of alternative techniques for inducing and controlling lucid dreams. While the previous chapters have already introduced you to some effective methods like reality testing, wake-initiated lucid dreaming (WILD), and mnemonic-induced lucid dreaming (MILD), the world of lucid dreaming is vast and offers a multitude of approaches to unlock the extraordinary potential of your dreams.

In this chapter, we invite you to expand your horizons and discover additional techniques that may resonate with you on a deeper level. By exploring these alternative methods, you will have a broader range of options to choose from, allowing you to tailor your lucid dreaming practice to suit your personal preferences, experiences, and unique dream landscape.

Lucid dreaming is a profoundly personal and subjective experience, and what works for one individual may not work as effectively for another. Therefore, it's essential to explore different techniques and find the ones that align best with your inclinations, beliefs, and desired outcomes. This chapter will serve as a comprehensive guide, introducing you to the Wake-Back-to-Bed (WBTB) technique, Finger Induced Lucid Dreaming (FILD), and several advanced methods that offer intriguing possibilities for lucid dream induction and exploration.

Lucid dreaming, as we have learned, holds tremendous potential for self-discovery, creativity, healing, and personal growth. By broadening your understanding of lucid dreaming techniques, you open doors to new possibilities and increase your chances of experiencing lucidity within your dreamscape. Each technique we will explore in this chapter comes with its own unique advantages, considerations, and nuances, allowing you to approach lucid dreaming from different angles and uncover what resonates most with you.

Whether you are a beginner just starting your lucid dreaming journey or an experienced dream explorer seeking fresh insights and techniques, this chapter will provide valuable information and guidance. We encourage you to keep an open mind and embrace the diversity of techniques presented here. Remember that lucid dreaming is a dynamic and ever-evolving practice, and what may seem challenging or elusive at first can become a profound and transformative experience with dedication and persistence.

In the upcoming sections, we will delve into the Wake-Back-to-Bed (WBTB) technique, where briefly waking up during the night can significantly increase your chances of experiencing lucid dreams. We will explore the optimal timing, strategies, and potential challenges associated with this technique. Additionally, we will introduce you to the Finger Induced Lucid Dreaming (FILD) technique, which offers a unique and simple approach to inducing lucidity through subtle finger movements.

Furthermore, we will delve into advanced lucid dreaming techniques that go beyond the traditional methods discussed earlier in the book. These advanced techniques include Dream Yoga, a spiritual practice rooted in Tibetan Buddhism that combines mindfulness and lucid dreaming to explore the nature of reality and consciousness. We will explore the philosophy, techniques, and potential benefits of dream yoga, providing you with insights into this transformative approach.

Additionally, we will discuss the use of subliminal messaging, supplements, herbs, and technological aids as tools to enhance your lucid dreaming practice. These alternative methods offer intriguing possibilities, but it's crucial to approach them with caution and an understanding of their potential benefits and risks.

By venturing into these alternative techniques, you will expand your repertoire of tools and strategies for lucid dreaming. Remember that lucid dreaming is a personal journey, and the most effective techniques will be those that resonate with your unique preferences and experiences. Experimentation and self-exploration are key, so take the time to explore different techniques, adapt them to your needs, and integrate them into your lucid dreaming practice.

In the following sections, we will guide you through each technique, providing detailed instructions, tips, and insights to support you on your lucid dreaming journey. Let us now embark together on this exciting exploration of alternative techniques for lucid dreaming, where hidden realms of consciousness and boundless possibilities await.

WAKE-BACK-TO-BED (WBTB) TECHNIQUE

The Wake-Back-to-Bed (WBTB) technique is a popular and effective method for inducing lucid dreams. It involves briefly waking up during the night and then returning to sleep with the intention of becoming lucid in the subsequent dream. By incorporating the WBTB technique into your practice, you can take advantage of the natural patterns of sleep and increase your chances of experiencing vivid and lucid dreams.

To successfully practice the WBTB technique, it is essential to understand the optimal timing for waking up and the subsequent period of wakefulness before returning to sleep. The timing of your WBTB attempt plays a significant role in its effectiveness. The general recommendation is to wake up during the latter portion of your sleep cycle, typically around 4-6 hours after falling asleep. This timing ensures that you have already experienced several cycles of rapid eye movement (REM) sleep, during which dreams are more frequent and vivid.

Upon waking up, it's important to resist the temptation to engage in stimulating activities that may hinder your ability to fall back asleep. Instead, maintain a calm and relaxed state of mind, as this will facilitate a smoother transition into the dream world. You can use this period of wakefulness to engage in gentle stretching, light reading, or meditation to promote a sense of relaxation and mental clarity.

During the wakeful period, it is beneficial to focus your mind on the intention of becoming lucid in your upcoming dreams. You can reaffirm this intention through affirmations, visualizations, or other mental exercises that reinforce your desire for lucidity. By actively directing your attention toward lucid dreaming, you enhance the likelihood of achieving it when you return to sleep.

When you feel ready to return to sleep, ensure that your sleep environment is conducive to relaxation and minimal disturbance. Dim the lights, adjust the temperature to your comfort, and create a soothing atmosphere that promotes a sense of tranquility. It may also be helpful to play soft, ambient music or use white noise machines to drown out external disturbances and maintain a calm environment.

As you lay in bed and prepare to drift back to sleep, it can be beneficial to employ relaxation techniques such as deep breathing, progressive muscle relaxation, or guided imagery. These practices help calm the mind and body, allowing for a smoother transition into the dream state. As you relax, maintain your focus on the intention of becoming lucid, visualizing yourself becoming aware within your dreams.

Once you have successfully transitioned back into sleep, be open to the experience of lucidity. It's important to cultivate a state of awareness while in the dream world to recognize the signs and cues that indicate you are dreaming. Reality checks, such as examining your hands, questioning your surroundings, or attempting to levitate, can serve as powerful triggers to initiate lucidity.

While the WBTB technique has proven to be highly effective for many individuals, it's essential to be patient and persistent. Lucid dreaming is a skill that develops with practice, and each attempt, even if it doesn't result in immediate lucidity, contributes to your overall progress. Keep a dream journal by your bedside to record any dreams or fragments you recall upon waking. Over time, this practice will improve your dream recall and help you identify patterns and themes within your dreams.

It's worth noting that the WBTB technique may disrupt your sleep schedule, especially if you consistently wake up during the night. Therefore, it's important to assess your individual circumstances and consider the potential impact on your overall sleep quality. If you find that the WBTB technique significantly disrupts your sleep or leaves you feeling excessively tired during the day, you may need to adjust the frequency or timing of your attempts to strike a balance between the benefits of lucid dreaming and maintaining overall well-being.

In conclusion, the Wake-Back-to-Bed (WBTB) technique is a powerful tool for inducing lucid dreams. By strategically waking up during the night and engaging in a period of wakefulness before returning to sleep, you can tap into the optimal conditions for lucidity. Through relaxation techniques, focused intention, and cultivating awareness, you increase your chances of experiencing vivid and lucid dreams. Remember to be patient and persistent, and maintain a journal to track your progress. With dedication and practice, the WBTB technique can become a valuable asset in your lucid dreaming toolkit.

FINGER INDUCED LUCID DREAMING (FILD) TECHNIQUE

The Finger Induced Lucid Dreaming (FILD) technique is a unique and accessible method for inducing lucid dreams. It involves subtle finger movements performed during the transition from wakefulness to sleep, allowing you to enter the dream state while maintaining a heightened level of awareness. The FILD technique has gained popularity among lucid dreamers due to its simplicity and effectiveness.

To practice the FILD technique, it's important to create a conducive sleep environment that promotes relaxation and minimizes distractions. Ensure that your sleeping space is comfortable, free from excessive noise or light, and at a temperature conducive to sleep. A calm and peaceful atmosphere will enhance your ability to enter the dream state with heightened awareness.

As you prepare to practice the FILD technique, find a comfortable position in bed and close your eyes. Take a few moments to focus on your breath, allowing your body and mind to relax. The goal is to enter a state of deep relaxation while maintaining a level of mental alertness.

Once you feel relaxed, bring your attention to your fingers. Start by placing your index and middle fingers lightly on the mattress or pillow beside you. The key to the FILD technique lies in the subtle movements of these two fingers. Begin to tap your fingers gently, almost as if you were playing a piano, without exerting any force or strain. The movements should be light and delicate, as if you were brushing your fingers across the surface.

As you tap your fingers, maintain a relaxed and focused state of mind. Allow your thoughts to flow freely without attaching them to any particular idea or concept. The gentle movements of your fingers serve as an anchor, keeping you connected to your physical body while your mind begins to drift into a dream state.

As you continue tapping your fingers, pay close attention to the sensations and subtle changes that occur. Be mindful of any shifts in perception, bodily sensations, or emerging dream imagery. The goal is to maintain a delicate balance between relaxation and awareness, allowing your mind to enter the dream world while remaining conscious of the experience.

After a period of tapping your fingers, you may start to notice a shift in your consciousness. You may experience a sense of floating, shifting sensations, or a general shift in your perception. These signs indicate that you are entering the dream state while maintaining awareness—an essential aspect of lucid dreaming.

Once you recognize the transition into the dream state, it's important to stabilize your lucidity. Take a moment to ground yourself in your dream environment. Engage your senses by observing your surroundings, feeling the texture of objects, or listening to the sounds within the dream. This active engagement helps solidify your lucidity and establish a firm connection to the dream world.

To prolong your lucid dream experience, it can be helpful to engage in activities that promote stability and control. Some lucid dreamers find success by spinning their dream bodies, rubbing their hands together, or chanting affirmations to maintain their lucidity. Experiment with different techniques to find what works best for you in sustaining your lucid dream state.

It's important to note that the FILD technique may not result in immediate lucidity for everyone. Like any lucid dreaming technique, it requires practice, patience, and experimentation. Each individual's experience with the FILD technique may vary, and it's essential to adapt the method to suit your unique preferences and physiology.

In addition to the physical practice of finger movements, mental preparation and intention-setting play a crucial role in the success of the FILD technique. Before initiating the finger tapping, take a moment to reaffirm your intention to become lucid within the dream. Visualize yourself becoming aware, mentally repeating affirmations such as "I am lucid in my dreams" or "I am aware within the dream state." This mental conditioning primes your subconscious mind for lucidity, increasing the likelihood of achieving a lucid dream through the FILD technique.

It's worth mentioning that the FILD technique is most effective when practiced during the early morning hours, when REM sleep cycles are more frequent and dreams tend to be more vivid. Experiment with different timings and variations of the technique to find what works best for you. Keep a dream journal by your bedside to record any lucid dreams or dream fragments that result from your FILD attempts. This practice not only helps you track your progress but also enhances your dream recall and self-awareness within the dream state.

In conclusion, the Finger Induced Lucid Dreaming (FILD) technique is a simple yet powerful method for inducing lucid dreams. By engaging in subtle finger movements during the transition from wakefulness to sleep, you can enter the dream state with heightened awareness. The FILD technique requires a combination of physical practice, mental preparation, and timing to achieve optimal results. Experiment with the technique, adapt it to suit your preferences, and maintain a journal to track your progress. With dedication and perseverance, the FILD technique can open the doors to fascinating and lucid dream experiences.

FINDING THE BEST TECHNIQUE FOR YOU

Lucid dreaming is a highly personal and subjective experience, and what works for one individual may not work for another. In this section, we will explore various factors to consider when choosing the best technique for inducing lucid dreams that aligns with your preferences, abilities, and lifestyle.

- **Self-Awareness:** Before delving into different techniques, it's crucial to develop a strong sense of self-awareness. Take time to reflect on your sleeping patterns, dream recall, and overall sleep quality. Are you a light sleeper or a heavy sleeper? Do you remember your dreams upon waking up? Understanding your sleep tendencies will help you choose a technique that complements your natural sleep patterns.

- **Time and Commitment:** Lucid dreaming requires time and commitment. Some techniques, such as Wake-Back-to-Bed (WBTB) and Finger Induced Lucid Dreaming (FILD), may disrupt your sleep schedule, requiring you to wake up during the night or engage in specific practices during the transition to sleep. Consider your daily routine, work commitments, and personal obligations when selecting a technique that you can consistently practice without significant interference.
- **Personal Preferences:** Different techniques appeal to different individuals based on their preferences and comfort levels. Some people enjoy the simplicity and gentle nature of reality testing, while others thrive on more advanced techniques like wake-initiated lucid dreaming (WILD). Consider whether you prefer a technique that incorporates physical actions, mental focus, or a combination of both. Choose a technique that resonates with you and aligns with your personal inclinations.
- **Skill Level:** Some techniques require more experience and skill to master than others. If you are a beginner in the world of

lucid dreaming, it may be beneficial to start with simpler techniques like reality testing or mnemonic-induced lucid dreaming (MILD). These techniques provide a solid foundation for understanding the basics of lucid dreaming and increasing your dream awareness. As you gain more experience and confidence, you can gradually explore and experiment with more advanced techniques.

- **Intention and Purpose:** Clarify your intention and purpose for lucid dreaming. Are you seeking creative inspiration, personal growth, problem-solving, or simply the joy of exploration? Different techniques may lend themselves better to specific intentions. For example, the Mnemonic-Induced Lucid Dreaming (MILD) technique is often used for setting intentions and affirmations, while the Wake-Initiated Lucid Dreaming (WILD) technique may provide more profound and immersive experiences. Align your technique selection with your desired outcomes.
- **Flexibility and adaptability:** Be open to adjusting and adapting techniques based on your individual needs. What works for you initially may change over time as

your understanding and skills develop. Remain flexible and willing to experiment with different techniques and variations to find what works best for you at different stages of your lucid dreaming practice. As you grow and evolve, your technique preferences may evolve as well.

- **Support and Resources:** Take advantage of the abundant resources available for lucid dreaming. Books, online forums, communities, and guided meditations can provide valuable insights, tips, and support as you navigate your lucid dreaming journey. Engage with like-minded individuals, share experiences, and seek guidance when needed. Having a support system can enhance your motivation, offer new perspectives, and help troubleshoot any challenges you encounter.

Remember, the journey of lucid dreaming is deeply personal, and there is no one-size-fits-all approach. Embrace the process of self-discovery, adaptability, and exploration as you find the technique that resonates with you the most. It may take time and practice to discover your preferred method, but the rewards of experiencing lucid dreams and unlocking the vast potential of your dream world are well worth the effort.

In conclusion, finding the best technique for inducing lucid dreams is a matter of self-awareness, personal preferences, commitment, and adaptability. Consider your sleep tendencies, daily routine, skill level, and desired outcomes when selecting a technique. Stay open to experimentation and be willing to adjust your approach as you progress in your lucid dreaming practice. Engage with resources and seek support from the lucid dreaming community to enhance your knowledge and motivation. With patience, perseverance, and the right technique, you can embark on an exciting and transformative journey within the realm of lucid dreaming.

CONCLUSION

In this chapter, we have explored alternative techniques for inducing and controlling lucid dreams. The Wake-Back-to-Bed (WBTB) technique, Finger Induced Lucid Dreaming (FILD), as well as advanced methods like Dream Yoga, subliminal messaging, supplements and herbs, and technological aids, offer a rich tapestry of possibilities for you to explore on your lucid dreaming journey. Each technique has its own unique advantages and considerations, and by experimenting with different approaches, you can find the methods that resonate most with you.

As you continue your exploration of lucid dreaming, remember that patience, persistence, and a genuine curiosity for the inner workings of your mind are key. Embrace the process and adapt your practice to suit your individual needs and experiences. The realm of lucid dreaming holds immense potential for self-discovery, creativity, and personal growth. With the techniques discussed in this chapter and throughout the book, you are equipped with the tools to embark on a transformative journey into the world of lucidity.

Part III

The Power of Lucid Dreaming

CHAPTER 8

Creative Expression through Lucid Dreaming

INTRODUCTION

Within the realm of lucid dreaming lies a powerful tool for unlocking creativity and artistic expression—a world where the boundaries of reality blur and the infinite reaches of the imagination are unleashed. Lucid dreams hold the promise of a vast canvas where the artist's mind can roam free, where ideas can take shape, and where the extraordinary becomes attainable. In this chapter, we embark on a journey to explore the profound connection between lucid dreaming and creative expression, delving into the ways in which lucid dreams can serve as a playground for artistic exploration, igniting the spark of inspiration and propelling the artist's craft to new heights.

Art has long been a medium through which human beings seek to express their deepest emotions, inner visions, and imaginative impulses. It is a means of transcending the limitations of the physical world and delving into the realms of the intangible, the abstract, and the sublime. Artists throughout history have pushed the boundaries of their respective disciplines, challenging conventions and reshaping the artistic landscape. In the pursuit of creative expression, artists often seek to access altered states of consciousness and tap into the wellspring of inspiration that lies beyond the confines of everyday awareness. Lucid dreaming offers a unique pathway to these altered states, opening up a realm where the ordinary becomes extraordinary and the unimaginable becomes attainable.

When we enter a lucid dream, we awaken within the dream itself, becoming conscious participants in the unfolding narrative. We gain the ability to shape the dream world and mold it according to our desires and artistic inclinations. The dream world becomes a vast playground where the laws of physics can be bent or disregarded entirely, where new horizons can be explored, and where the constraints of reality fade away. In this realm of limitless possibilities, the creative mind finds fertile ground to sow the seeds of inspiration and harvest the fruits of imagination.

It is in lucid dreams that artists can engage their senses in profound ways. The dream world presents a heightened sensory experience where colors are more vibrant, sounds are more resonant, and textures are more palpable. Visual artists can drink in the vivid hues of dreamscapes, capturing ethereal landscapes or abstract visions that transcend the boundaries of what the waking world can offer. Writers can immerse themselves in the intricate tapestry of the dream world, capturing its essence through evocative prose that transports readers to unseen realms. Musicians can listen to the symphony of the dream, composing melodies that echo the otherworldly harmonies they encounter within the lucid dream state.

Within the lucid dream, artists have at their disposal a unique toolbox, one that defies the limitations of the physical world. Paintbrushes that bring color to life with a mere thought, sculpting clay that molds effortlessly under their fingertips, musical instruments that produce ethereal melodies at the slightest touch—the dream world offers an abundance of creative instruments that can be summoned with a mere intention. As artists wield these tools within the dream, they can explore and experiment, bringing their visions to life in ways that transcend the constraints of the waking world. The dream world becomes an artist's sanctuary, a realm where ideas can be birthed, nurtured, and brought to fruition.

The lucid dreamer is not alone in this creative exploration. Within the dream world, an entire cast of characters awaits collaboration. Dream figures, whether fantastical or mundane, can serve as artistic collaborators, offering guidance, inspiration, or even critique. Engaging in conversations with dream characters allows artists to tap into the collective wisdom of the dream world, drawing upon the creative wellspring that lies within each character. These interactions can spark new ideas, illuminate unexplored artistic paths, and foster unexpected collaborations that enrich the artistic journey.

For artists who encounter creative blocks and stagnation, lucid dreaming can be a transformative tool for breaking through these barriers. By setting intentions before entering a lucid dream, artists can directly address creative obstacles, seeking guidance from the dream itself. In the dream state, barriers can be dissolved and new perspectives can emerge, freeing the artist from the constraints that hinder their creative flow. Lucid dreaming becomes a sanctuary for rejuvenation, an incubator for fresh ideas, and a springboard for creative growth.

But lucid dreaming is not confined to the dream world alone. It transcends the boundaries of sleep and reverberates within the waking life of the artist. Many artists have harnessed the inspiration and insights gained from lucid dreaming to shape their artistic endeavors in the physical world. Architects have designed breathtaking structures born from dream visions; dancers have choreographed ethereal movements inspired by their dream experiences; and filmmakers have transformed surreal dreamscapes into captivating visual narratives. Lucid dreaming becomes a conduit for bringing artistic visions to life, a laboratory for experimentation, and a source of inspiration that fuels the creative process.

Throughout history, visionary artists have drawn upon their dream experiences to create works that captivate and challenge our perceptions of reality. From the surrealist paintings of Salvador Dal, where melting clocks and fragmented dreamscapes evoke the surreal nature of dreams, to the dream-inspired literature of Haruki Murakami, where mundane reality intertwines with the ethereal realms of the subconscious, these artists have tapped into the wellspring of the dream world to shape their artistic legacy. By incorporating the visions, symbolism, and emotions evoked by their lucid dreams, these artists have enriched the artistic landscape and invited audiences to embark on a journey beyond the confines of ordinary existence.

In this chapter, we embark on a voyage through the dreamscape, exploring the myriad ways in which lucid dreaming intersects with the realms of artistic expression. We delve into the techniques and practices that empower artists to tap into the creative potential of lucid dreams, from harnessing the senses to collaborating with dream characters. We examine how lucid dreaming can break through creative blocks, serve as a platform for prototyping artistic projects, and inspire artists to transcend the limits of their craft. By unlocking the door to the dream world, artists unlock the door to boundless inspiration, limitless possibilities, and a journey of creative exploration that knows no bounds.

Join us as we delve into the power of creative expression through lucid dreaming, an exploration that invites artists of all disciplines to venture beyond the ordinary, transcend the constraints of reality, and embark on an artistic odyssey that extends into the realm of dreams. Together, let us unlock the creative potential that lies dormant within and awaken to the wondrous possibilities that await in the embrace of lucid dreaming.

THE LIBERATION OF THE CREATIVE MIND

Creativity is a boundless force that resides within every individual, eager to find expression and manifest in various forms. Yet, in the hustle and bustle of everyday life, the creative mind often finds itself constrained by the limitations and expectations of the world. This is where lucid dreaming emerges as a transformative gateway, offering liberation and a sanctuary for the creative spirit to roam free.

In the realm of lucid dreaming, the artist's mind becomes unshackled from the constraints of the physical world. As we enter a lucid dream, we awaken within the dream itself, stepping into a vivid alternate reality where the ordinary becomes extraordinary and the unimaginable becomes possible. In this state of awareness, we are endowed with the power to shape the dream world, to bend its rules to our creative whims, and to explore realms beyond the confines of everyday existence.

The experience of lucid dreaming is akin to entering a vast playground where the boundaries of reality dissolve. Within this boundless playground, artists find themselves immersed in breathtaking dreamscapes, traversing awe-inspiring landscapes, encountering mythical creatures, and venturing into uncharted territories limited only by the expanses of the imagination. It is within these ethereal dreamscapes that the artist's mind is liberated, free to explore, experiment, and indulge in a cornucopia of sensory experiences that are more vivid and immersive than anything the waking world can offer.

Visual artists find themselves surrounded by vibrant colors, textures, and shapes that seem to pulsate with a vibrancy beyond comprehension. The hues of a sunset cascade across the sky in a symphony of warm tones, while the cool touch of dew-kissed petals resonates through the fingertips. The dream world becomes a living canvas upon which the artist can paint their visions, capturing the essence of dreams and channeling it onto physical mediums.

Writers, too, are enraptured by the boundless possibilities of lucid dreaming. In this realm, the written word transcends the boundaries of the mundane, becoming a vehicle to express the ineffable beauty and complexity of the dream experience. The descriptive power of language becomes amplified, enabling writers to vividly convey the sights, sounds, scents, and emotions that permeate the dream world. Through lucid dreaming, writers find themselves endowed with an endless well of inspiration, weaving narratives that blur the lines between reality and fantasy, awakening readers to the infinite realms of the imagination.

Musicians, in the embrace of lucid dreaming, tap into a symphony of otherworldly sounds. The ethereal melodies that resonate within dreams defy the limitations of conventional instruments, evoking emotions that transcend the constraints of everyday life. In this state of creative liberation, musicians find themselves composing haunting melodies, experimental arrangements, and harmonies that echo the very essence of the dream world. The dream becomes a stage where the artist can orchestrate their innermost emotions and transcend the confines of traditional composition.

Within the lucid dream, the artist is not merely an observer but an active participant, shaping the dream narrative and engaging with the dream figures that populate the dreamscapes. Dream characters, whether fantastical or mundane, become artistic collaborators, offering insights, inspiration, and a mirror to reflect the depths of the artist's psyche. Conversations with dream characters reveal hidden aspects of the self, unlocking new perspectives and enriching the artistic journey. Through these interactions, artists gain access to the collective wisdom of the dream world, drawing upon the creative wellspring that resides within each character encountered.

Moreover, lucid dreaming serves as a sanctuary for artists to confront and transcend creative blocks that may impede their artistic journey. These blocks can arise from self-doubt, fear, or a lack of inspiration. However, within the realm of lucid dreaming, artists can directly address these obstacles, seeking guidance and resolution from the dream itself. Lucid dreams become a playground for experimentation, a space where artists can push the boundaries of their craft, test new ideas, and find innovative solutions to artistic challenges.

Beyond the dream world, lucid dreaming infuses waking life with renewed inspiration and fresh perspectives. Artists harness the insights gained from lucid dreaming, infusing their creative projects with a touch of the extraordinary. Architects design buildings inspired by the visionary structures encountered in their lucid dreams, challenging conventional notions of form and function. Choreographers translate the fluid movements of dreamscapes into mesmerizing dance routines that defy gravity and stretch the boundaries of physicality. Filmmakers draw upon the surreal landscapes of their lucid dreams, capturing the essence of the dream world on the silver screen and captivating audiences with visual narratives that blur the lines between reality and fantasy.

Throughout history, visionary artists have looked to the realm of dreams for inspiration, often blurring the boundaries between the dream world and waking life. The surrealists, with Salvador Dal at the forefront, embraced the transformative power of dreams, channeling the symbolic, bizarre, and unconscious elements of their dreams into their artwork. Dal's paintings, such as "The Persistence of Memory," with their melting clocks and distorted landscapes, invite viewers to ponder the enigmatic nature of dreams and the vastness of the creative mind.

Similarly, the realm of literature has been enriched by authors who have ventured into the depths of their dreams. Haruki Murakami, a master of dream-like narratives, often draws upon his own dreams as a source of inspiration. In works such as "Kafka on the Shore," he weaves together dreams and reality, creating a seamless tapestry that blurs the boundaries between the conscious and unconscious realms. Murakami's prose invites readers to embark on a literary journey that transcends the limitations of the physical world, delving into the realms of the psyche and the power of the imagination.

In the fusion of the dream world and artistic expression, artists find themselves liberated from the constraints of reality, transcending the limits of their medium, and unearthing the deepest recesses of their creative potential. The freedom and expansiveness of lucid dreaming serve as catalysts for artistic growth, enabling artists to break free from creative stagnation, explore uncharted territories, and embrace the full spectrum of their creative capabilities.

In the following sections of this chapter, we will explore the techniques and practices that empower artists to harness the creative potential of lucid dreaming. From cultivating a heightened sense of awareness within the dream to engaging in collaborative ventures with dream characters, artists will discover a myriad of tools to unlock their artistic potential within the realm of lucid dreaming.

Furthermore, we will delve into how lucid dreaming can serve as a platform for prototyping artistic projects, refining artistic visions, and expanding the boundaries of what is possible within their respective disciplines.

Join us on this transformative journey through the interplay of lucid dreaming and creative expression. Together, let us liberate the creative mind, venture into uncharted artistic territories, and discover the infinite wellspring of inspiration that lies within the embrace of lucid dreaming.

EXPLORING THE DREAMSCAPES

Within the realm of lucid dreaming lies a vast expanse of dreamscapes waiting to be explored. These dreamscapes, like uncharted territories, hold untold wonders, mysteries, and infinite possibilities for artistic exploration. They serve as canvases upon which artists can paint with the colors of imagination, sculpt with the textures of emotions, and compose with the symphony of inspiration. In this section, we embark on a journey to navigate dreamscapes, discovering the techniques and practices that enable artists to fully immerse themselves in the rich tapestry of the dream world.

As artists venture into dreamscapes, the first step is to cultivate a heightened sense of awareness within the dream. This state of lucidity allows artists to engage with their dreams consciously, fully experiencing and interacting with the dream environment. Through reality testing techniques practiced in waking life, such as regularly questioning one's reality, performing reality checks, and cultivating mindfulness, artists develop the ability to recognize the dream state, triggering the onset of lucidity.

Once lucidity is achieved, artists find themselves standing at the threshold of limitless creative potential. The dreamscapes beckon, inviting them to explore landscapes that defy the laws of physics, encounter extraordinary beings, and witness breathtaking vistas that transcend the imagination. Artists may find themselves soaring through the skies, feeling the exhilarating rush of wind against their faces, or plunging into the depths of an underwater realm, marveling at the vibrant colors and exotic creatures that inhabit the dream waters. The dreamscapes become a playground for sensory exploration, where every sight, sound, touch, taste, and smell is heightened, intensifying the artistic experience.

Within dreamscapes, artists may encounter dream characters who can serve as collaborators, guides, or sources of inspiration. These dream characters are extensions of the artist's subconscious, representing aspects of their psyche and creative potential. Engaging in conversations with dream characters opens doors to new perspectives, insights, and creative ideas. Artists may seek advice from wise dream mentors, engage in artistic collaborations with dream figures who possess unique talents, or simply observe the behavior of dream characters to gain a deeper understanding of their own artistic process.

The dreamscapes also provide artists with an opportunity to experiment with different artistic mediums and techniques. The dream world becomes a living laboratory where artists can test new ideas, push the boundaries of their craft, and explore unconventional artistic expressions. Painters may find themselves effortlessly creating vivid and intricate artworks using colors that transcend the limitations of the physical palette. Sculptors can mold dream matter into intricate forms, shaping ethereal sculptures that defy the constraints of gravity. Musicians may compose symphonies that evoke the essence of the dream world, combining unfamiliar melodies and otherworldly sounds to create hauntingly beautiful compositions. In dreamscapes, the possibilities for artistic experimentation are boundless.

Moreover, artists can utilize lucid dreaming as a means to refine their artistic visions and gain clarity in their creative endeavors. By revisiting and revising artistic projects within the dream, artists can explore different perspectives, experiment with alternative approaches, and refine their artistic expressions. Whether it's fine-tuning a brushstroke, rewriting a scene, or reimagining a dance sequence, dreamscapes offer a sanctuary for artistic refinement, enabling artists to tap into their intuition, instincts, and the collective wisdom of the dream world.

The dreamscapes also hold hidden symbols, archetypes, and themes that can inspire profound artistic creations. Artists may encounter recurring symbols or themes within their lucid dreams, which serve as potent sources of inspiration and avenues for personal exploration. These symbols may carry deep personal meanings or resonate with universal themes that captivate audiences. By delving into the symbolism of their dreams, artists can infuse their creative works with layers of depth and evoke powerful emotional responses in their viewers or listeners.

In the fusion of the conscious artist's mind and the subconscious dreamscapes, a symbiotic relationship emerges. Lucid dreaming nourishes the artistic soul, providing an endless wellspring of inspiration, while the artist's creative spirit infuses the dream world with intention and purpose. This interplay between the artist and the dreamscapes allows for the co-creation of artistic experiences that transcend the boundaries of the waking world.

As artists explore dreamscapes, they are encouraged to keep dream journals, recording their dream experiences, insights, and artistic inspirations. These dream journals become treasure troves of artistic material, serving as references for future projects and providing a rich source of ideas and themes. By revisiting dream journal entries, artists can delve into the depths of their dreamscapes, unearthing forgotten memories, rekindling dormant inspirations, and immersing themselves in the ever-expanding universe of the dream world.

In conclusion, the dreamscapes hold a myriad of artistic possibilities, waiting to be explored by the intrepid artist. Within these ethereal realms, artists can cultivate lucidity, engage with dream characters, experiment with artistic mediums and techniques, refine their artistic visions, and draw inspiration from the profound symbolism and themes encountered within their dreams. The dreamscapes offer a sanctuary for the artistic soul, a realm where the artist's imagination knows no bounds and where the fusion of dreams and artistry gives rise to transformative and awe-inspiring creations. So, step into the dreamscapes, unlock the door to your creative potential, and let the dream world be your muse.

HARNESSING THE SENSES

In the realm of lucid dreaming, the senses come alive in ways that surpass the limitations of the physical world. The dreamscapes become a playground for the artist's senses, where colors are more vibrant, sounds are more resonant, textures are more tangible, tastes are more tantalizing, and scents are more evocative. In this section, we delve into the art of harnessing the senses within lucid dreaming, exploring how artists can fully immerse themselves in the rich sensory tapestry of the dream world and translate these experiences into their creative expressions.

Visual artistry takes on a whole new dimension within the dreamscapes. Artists find themselves surrounded by a kaleidoscope of colors, textures, and forms that defy the boundaries of the physical realm. Vivid hues burst forth with a vibrancy that seems to pulsate with life, beckoning the artist to capture their essence. Artists can observe the interplay of light and shadow, the ethereal landscapes that stretch into the horizon, and the intricate details that elude the waking eye. Within the dreamscapes, the artist's vision becomes heightened, allowing for a deeper appreciation of the visual intricacies that define their artistic style.

To fully harness the visual sense within lucid dreaming, artists can employ techniques such as focusing their attention on specific visual elements or actively shaping the dream environment to suit their artistic desires. By honing their ability to maintain lucidity and clarity of vision, artists can bring dreamscapes to life with breathtaking detail, capturing the essence of their dreams through visual mediums such as painting, drawing, photography, or digital art. The dream world becomes a vast source of inspiration, where artists can channel surreal landscapes, mythical creatures, and fantastical scenarios into their artistic creations.

Soundscapes within the dreamscapes offer a symphony of auditory experiences that surpass the limitations of the physical realm. Artists find themselves enveloped in ethereal melodies, rhythmic beats, and harmonious compositions that resonate deep within their souls. The dreamscapes amplify the artist's ability to perceive and appreciate the nuances of sound, enabling them to distinguish between the faintest whispers, the crescendo of a thunderous orchestra, or the delicate rustling of leaves in a gentle breeze.

To harness the auditory sense within lucid dreaming, artists can actively engage with the soundscape of their dreams. They can listen intently to the music that permeates the dream world, actively participate in its composition, or even create their own melodies and harmonies. Musicians can play imaginary instruments, conduct dream orchestras, or sing with celestial voices, immersing themselves in the symphony of dreamscapes. By embracing the auditory sensations within the dream, artists can translate these ethereal sounds into musical compositions, sound installations, or even incorporate them into spoken word performances or storytelling.

The dreamscapes are not just a visual and auditory feast but also a playground for the sense of touch. In lucid dreams, artists can experience tactile sensations that defy the boundaries of the physical world. They can feel the softness of petals against their skin, the coolness of water as it cascades over their fingertips, or the warmth of a gentle caress from a dream character. The dream world invites artists to explore textures, shapes, and forms that are beyond the realm of waking reality, allowing them to fully immerse themselves in a multisensory experience.

To harness the sense of touch within lucid dreaming, artists can actively engage with the dream environment through tactile exploration. They can run their fingers over dream surfaces, feel the weight and texture of dream objects, or even shape dream matter with their hands. This heightened sense of touch opens up avenues for artistic expression, enabling sculptors to mold dream matter into intricate forms, textile artists to feel the intricate weaves of dream fabrics, or dancers to experience the flow of movement as they gracefully traverse the dreamscapes.

The sense of taste in lucid dreaming offers a tantalizing opportunity for artistic exploration. Artists can indulge in the most delectable flavors, savoring the taste of exotic fruits, culinary delights, or even imaginary concoctions. The dreamscapes awaken the artist's taste buds to new sensations as flavors explode on the palate with an intensity that surpasses the limitations of the physical world. Artists can immerse themselves in the culinary wonders of their dreams, drawing inspiration from the exotic tastes and flavors encountered within the dreamscapes.

To harness the sense of taste within lucid dreaming, artists can actively engage with the culinary experiences offered by the dream world. They can experiment with flavors, concoct imaginary recipes, or even dine with dream characters, exploring the vast array of tastes that exist within the realm of dreams. This sensory exploration can inspire culinary artists, food photographers, or writers to capture the essence of these dream flavors in their creative works, enticing audiences to embark on a gastronomic journey that transcends the boundaries of the physical palate.

The sense of smell in lucid dreaming evokes a world of olfactory sensations that transport artists to realms beyond the limitations of the physical realm. The dreamscapes are infused with scents that evoke nostalgia, mystery, or even a touch of the surreal. Artists find themselves enveloped in fragrances that stimulate memories, evoke emotions, or ignite the imagination. The dream world offers a rich tapestry of scents, from the delicate aroma of blooming flowers to the intoxicating scent of a distant bonfire, enticing artists to explore the olfactory landscape of their dreams.

To harness the sense of smell within lucid dreaming, artists can actively engage with the scents that permeate the dreamscapes. They can immerse themselves in the fragrance of dream flowers, inhale the aromas of dream landscapes, or even create their own scents within the dream. This olfactory exploration can inspire perfumers, visual artists, or writers to capture the essence of these dream scents in their creative works, evoking visceral responses and transporting audiences to realms that transcend the boundaries of the physical sense of smell.

In conclusion, the art of harnessing the senses within lucid dreaming offers artists a gateway to an immersive and multisensory creative experience. By fully engaging with the visual, auditory, tactile, gustatory, and olfactory sensations within the dreamscapes, artists can elevate their artistic expressions to new heights, capturing the essence of their dreams and infusing their creative works with a depth and richness that transcend the limitations of the physical world. The dreamscapes become a sanctuary where the artist's senses are enlivened, the boundaries of the imagination are expanded, and the artistic potential knows no bounds. So, step into the dreamscapes, immerse yourself in the sensory wonders that await, and let your artistic journey be guided by the symphony of senses within the realm of lucid dreaming.

THE LUCID DREAM ARTIST'S TOOLBOX

Within the realm of lucid dreaming, artists have access to a unique toolbox that empowers them to create and explore their artistic visions with unparalleled freedom. This toolbox is filled with techniques, practices, and resources specifically tailored to harness the creative potential of the dream world. In this section, we delve into the components of the Lucid Dream Artist's Toolbox, equipping artists with the necessary tools to unlock their artistic potential within the dreamscapes.

- **Dream Incubation:** Dream incubation is a powerful technique that allows artists to direct their dreams towards specific themes, subjects, or artistic goals. By focusing their intention and attention on a desired dream experience before sleep, artists can plant the seeds of inspiration within their subconscious mind. This technique involves setting clear intentions, visualizing desired dream scenarios, and affirming one's artistic intentions before sleep. Dream incubation serves as a catalyst for artistic exploration within the dreamscapes, providing a starting point and guiding the artist's creative journey.

- **Dream Recall and Journaling:** Dream recall and journaling are essential practices for artists to capture and preserve the ephemeral nature of their dream experiences. By developing the habit of recording dreams in a dream journal immediately upon waking, artists can retain vivid details, emotions, and artistic inspirations that emerge within the dreamscapes. Dream journaling not only serves as a repository of artistic material but also enhances dream recall over time, allowing artists to tap into the vast wealth of their dream experiences and extract artistic gems that might have otherwise been lost.
- **Creative Visualization:** Creative visualization is a technique that enables artists to mentally rehearse and envision artistic creations within the dream world. By vividly visualizing their desired artistic outcomes, artists can enhance their ability to manifest these visions within their dreamscapes. Creative visualization can be employed to rehearse artistic performances, imagine intricate details of visual artworks, or even visualize the creative process itself. This practice strengthens the connection between the artist's mind and

the dream world, laying the foundation for transformative artistic experiences.

- **Embodied Imagination:** Embodied imagination is a technique that encourages artists to embody and fully immerse themselves in the artistic experiences within dreamscapes. By engaging not only the mind but also the body, artists can deepen their connection with their artistic expressions. This technique involves physically engaging with dream objects, environments, and characters, allowing the artist to fully experience the sensations, movements, and emotions associated with their artistic creations. Through embodied imagination, artists can tap into the somatic aspects of their artistic expression, creating more authentic and visceral works.
- **Symbolism and Archetypes:** The dream world is rich with symbolism and archetypal imagery that holds profound meaning and inspiration for artists. By exploring the symbolic language of their dreams, artists can tap into the collective unconscious and draw upon universal themes that resonate deeply with audiences. Familiarizing oneself with common symbols and archetypes allows artists to interpret and utilize these powerful images within their

creative works, infusing their art with layers of depth and meaning that transcend the personal realm.

- **Collaborative Dreaming:** Collaborative dreaming involves consciously engaging with dream characters and entities within the dreamscapes, inviting them to become active participants in the artistic process. By seeking out dream collaborators, artists can engage in artistic dialogues, receive guidance, and even co-create artistic works within the dream world. These dream characters can provide unique perspectives, offer inspiration, or contribute their own creative input, enriching the artist's creative journey and expanding the artistic possibilities within the dreamscapes.
- **Time Manipulation:** Lucid dreaming offers artists the ability to manipulate time within their dreamscapes. This tool allows artists to extend the duration of their creative explorations, providing ample time for artistic experimentation, refinement, and reflection. By slowing down or elongating dream time, artists can delve deeper into their artistic process, explore intricate details, or even experience extended periods of artistic creation within a single dream. Time manipulation within

lucid dreaming liberates artists from the constraints of waking reality and empowers them to fully immerse themselves in the creative flow.

- **Dream Re-entry:** Dream re-entry is a technique that allows artists to revisit and continue dream experiences that were left unresolved or unfinished. This tool provides artists with the opportunity to explore different artistic paths, experiment with alternative creative outcomes, or deepen their understanding of specific dream themes or characters. By consciously re-entering dreams, artists can access dreamscapes with heightened lucidity and intention, engaging in artistic explorations that transcend the limitations of linear time.
- **Integration and Reflection:** Integration and reflection serve as essential components of the Lucid Dream Artist's Toolbox. After engaging in artistic explorations within dreamscapes, it is crucial for artists to integrate their dream experiences into their waking lives and reflect upon the insights and inspirations gained. This process involves contemplating the symbolism, emotions, and themes encountered within the dreams and translating them into

tangible artistic expressions. Integration and reflection allow artists to bridge the gap between the dream world and the waking world, infusing their artistic creations with the wisdom and transformative power of their dream experiences.

By incorporating these tools into their artistic practice, artists can unlock the full potential of lucid dreaming as a source of inspiration, exploration, and creative expression. The Lucid Dream Artist's Toolbox equips artists with a diverse array of techniques and practices that enable them to harness the limitless possibilities of dreamscapes, merging the realms of dreams and artistry into a transcendent creative journey. So, open your toolbox, embrace the artistic potential within your dreams, and let the power of lucid dreaming unleash your creative spirit.

COLLABORATING WITH DREAM CHARACTERS

Within the realm of lucid dreaming, one of the most fascinating aspects is the ability to engage and collaborate with the dream characters that inhabit the dreamscapes. These dream characters can serve as artistic allies, sources of inspiration, or even mentors within the creative journey. In this section, we delve into the art of collaborating with dream characters, exploring the profound impact they can have on an artist's creative process and the unique opportunities they present for artistic exploration.

- **Recognizing Dream Characters:** The first step in collaborating with dream characters is to become aware of their presence within the dreamscapes. Lucid dreaming provides the artist with the ability to consciously interact with these characters, recognizing them as distinct entities rather than mere figments of the imagination. By practicing self-awareness and reality testing techniques within the dream, artists can discern dream characters from the dream environment and initiate meaningful interactions.
- **Establishing Communication:** Once a dream character is recognized, establishing clear and effective communication becomes essential for collaboration. Dream characters may communicate through spoken words, telepathy, gestures, or even symbolic representations. Artists can practice active listening, engaging in dialogue, and asking open-ended questions to deepen their understanding of the dream characters' perspectives, motivations, and artistic insights. This exchange of ideas

and information forms the foundation for collaborative artistic endeavors within the dreamscapes.

- **Seeking Artistic Guidance**: Dream characters can serve as invaluable sources of artistic guidance, offering inspiration, feedback, and creative direction. Artists can seek out specific dream characters who possess artistic expertise or embody qualities that align with their artistic vision. These dream characters can provide guidance on artistic techniques, offer novel perspectives, or even share their own artistic creations within the dream. By actively seeking out artistic guidance from dream characters, artists can tap into a wellspring of artistic wisdom that transcends the limitations of waking reality.
- **Co-Creating Artworks:** Collaborating with dream characters opens up the possibility of co-creating artworks within the dreamscapes. Artists can invite dream characters to participate in artistic endeavors, whether it be painting, sculpting, dancing, or any other form of artistic expression. Dream characters can contribute their unique perspectives, creative input, or even showcase their own artistic talents, leading to truly collaborative

and multidimensional artworks that blend the artist's vision with the dream characters' contributions. This co-creation process expands the artistic possibilities within the dream world and fosters a sense of shared ownership and creativity.

- **Exploring Dreamscapes Together:** Dream characters can act as companions and guides, accompanying artists on explorations through the vast dreamscapes. By embarking on artistic adventures with dream characters, artists can discover hidden realms, encounter fantastical landscapes, and immerse themselves in extraordinary experiences that fuel their artistic imagination. Dream characters can provide insights, introduce the artist to new artistic influences, or even present challenges that push artistic boundaries. Exploring dreamscapes together with dream characters enhances the artist's creative journey and nurtures a sense of artistic camaraderie within the dream world.
- **Symbolic Interactions:** Dream characters often embody symbolic representations and archetypes that hold profound artistic meaning. By engaging with these symbolic interactions, artists can tap into the

collective unconscious and access universal themes that resonate deeply within their creative expressions. Dream characters may personify emotions, embody mythological figures, or represent aspects of the artist's psyche. Artists can explore these symbolic interactions, allowing them to gain insight into their own artistic process, explore personal themes, and infuse their creative works with layers of depth and symbolism.

- **Embracing Surprises and Serendipity:** Collaborating with dream characters necessitates embracing the unexpected and welcoming serendipitous moments within the dreamscapes. Dream characters can introduce unforeseen elements, initiate spontaneous artistic performances, or present opportunities for artistic experimentation that transcend the artist's conscious expectations. By embracing surprises and being open to the unexpected, artists can tap into the limitless creative potential of the dream world, allowing the artistic process to unfold in ways that surpass their preconceived notions.
- **Reflecting and Integrating:** After collaborating with dream characters, it is crucial for artists to reflect upon and integrate the artistic insights gained from

these interactions. This reflective process involves contemplating the experiences, emotions, and lessons encountered while collaborating with dream characters. Artists can journal about their collaborative experiences, create artworks inspired by the interactions, or incorporate the artistic contributions of dream characters into their waking artistic practice. Reflecting and integrating the collaborative experiences within the dreamscapes allows artists to bridge the gap between the dream world and the waking world, infusing their artistic creations with the wisdom and transformative power of their collaborative dream journeys.

Collaborating with dream characters within the realm of lucid dreaming unlocks a realm of artistic possibilities. These dream characters become artistic allies, mentors, and sources of inspiration, providing artists with a rich tapestry of perspectives, ideas, and insights. By recognizing dream characters, establishing effective communication, seeking guidance, co-creating artworks, exploring dreamscapes together, engaging in symbolic interactions, embracing surprises, and reflecting on the collaborative experiences, artists can tap into the extraordinary creative potential that lies within the collaborative realm of the dreamscapes. So, venture forth, engage with the dream characters that await, and let the power of collaboration within lucid dreaming propel your artistic journey to new heights.

TRANSCENDING CREATIVE BLOCKS

Creative blocks are a common challenge that artists encounter on their creative journey, regardless of whether they are awake or exploring the realms of lucid dreaming. These blocks can manifest as a lack of inspiration, self-doubt, or a feeling of being stuck in a creative rut. However, lucid dreaming provides unique opportunities to transcend these blocks and tap into a wellspring of creative energy and innovation. In this section, we explore various techniques and approaches that artists can employ within dreamscapes to overcome creative blocks and unleash their artistic potential.

- **Embracing Surrender and Letting Go:** One approach to transcending creative blocks within lucid dreaming is to embrace surrender and let go of preconceived notions or expectations. By surrendering to the flow of the dreamscapes and relinquishing control, artists can tap into the subconscious mind and access unexplored realms of creativity. This surrendering process involves releasing attachment to specific outcomes or judgments, allowing the dreamscapes to guide the artistic process and uncover hidden sources of inspiration.

- **Exploring New Perspectives:** Lucid dreaming offers artists the opportunity to explore new perspectives and alternative ways of seeing the world. By consciously shifting their point of view within the dreamscapes, artists can gain fresh insights, challenge conventional thinking, and break free from creative stagnation. Artists can experiment with viewing their artworks from different angles, exploring their creations through the eyes of dream characters, or even assuming the perspectives of inanimate objects. This exploration of new perspectives stimulates the creative mind and fosters innovative thinking.
- **Engaging in Playfulness and Experimentation:** Playfulness and experimentation are powerful tools for transcending creative blocks within lucid dreaming. Artists can embrace a sense of childlike wonder, curiosity, and joy as they navigate the dreamscapes. This mindset encourages the exploration of

unconventional artistic techniques, the fusion of different art forms, and the uninhibited expression of creativity. By engaging in playful experimentation, artists can break free from self-imposed limitations, discover new artistic territories, and rekindle the joy of creation.

- **Utilizing Dream Symbols and Metaphors:** Dream symbols and metaphors can serve as catalysts for transcending creative blocks within lucid dreaming. Artists can explore the symbolism and meaning behind dream imagery, allowing it to inspire and inform their artistic endeavors. By delving into the depths of the dream symbols and metaphors, artists can tap into the collective unconscious and access a wellspring of archetypal themes that resonate deeply with their creative expressions. This utilization of dream symbols and metaphors breathes new life into the artistic process and opens doors to unexplored creative possibilities.
- **Engaging in Collaborative Dreaming:** Collaborative dreaming, as discussed earlier, is not only a means of artistic collaboration but also a powerful tool for transcending creative blocks. Dream characters within the dreamscapes can offer insights, perspectives, and guidance that can help

artists overcome creative stagnation. By actively seeking out dream characters who embody qualities or expertise relevant to the artist's creative block, artists can receive support, inspiration, and fresh ideas that ignite their creative spark.

- **Harnessing the Power of Intention:** Intention plays a vital role in transcending creative blocks within lucid dreaming. Artists can set clear intentions before entering the dreamscapes, directing their focus toward overcoming specific creative challenges or breaking through artistic barriers. By consciously infusing their intention with a sense of determination, artists tap into the vast potential of their subconscious mind and create a fertile ground for creative breakthroughs. The power of intention within lucid dreaming propels the artist towards innovative solutions and fresh perspectives.
- **Embodying Creative Archetypes:** Lucid dreaming allows artists to embody and interact with various archetypal personas and figures within the dreamscapes. Artists can consciously assume the roles of creative archetypes such as the visionary, the muse, the trickster, or the alchemist, tapping into their inherent qualities and energy.

This embodiment of creative archetypes enables artists to access untapped reserves of inspiration, confidence, and artistic flow, bypassing creative blocks and unlocking their full creative potential.

- **Revisiting Past Artistic Challenges:** Lucid dreaming provides the opportunity to revisit past artistic challenges or unfinished projects with a fresh perspective. Artists can intentionally enter dream scenarios where they encounter past artworks or creative obstacles, allowing them to explore alternative approaches, experiment with new techniques, or find closure. This process of revisiting past challenges within the dreamscapes promotes artistic growth, facilitates problem-solving, and frees the artist from lingering creative blocks.
- **Journaling and Reflection:** Journaling and reflection serve as vital tools for transcending creative blocks within lucid dreaming. Artists can maintain a dream journal, documenting their lucid dream experiences, artistic insights, and breakthroughs. By reflecting on these journal entries, artists gain valuable self-awareness, identify patterns, and extract lessons that inform their waking artistic practice. Journaling and reflection within

lucid dreaming foster a deep connection with the creative self and provide a roadmap for transcending future creative blocks.

- **Integration and Action:** Finally, transcending creative blocks within lucid dreaming is incomplete without integration and taking action in the waking world. Artists must integrate the creative breakthroughs, insights, and inspirations gained from lucid dreaming into their daily artistic practice. This involves translating the dreamscapes' wisdom and energy into tangible artistic expressions, experimenting with new techniques or styles, or implementing innovative ideas into their creative works. Integration and action ensure that the transformative power of lucid dreaming is harnessed to its fullest extent, propelling artists beyond their creative blocks and into a realm of boundless artistic exploration.

By embracing surrender, exploring new perspectives, engaging in playfulness and experimentation, utilizing dream symbols and metaphors, practicing collaborative dreaming, harnessing the power of intention, embodying creative archetypes, revisiting past challenges, journaling and reflecting, and integrating the insights gained from lucid dreaming into their waking artistic practice, artists can transcend creative blocks and unlock their limitless artistic potential. Lucid dreaming becomes a transformative space where creative stagnation gives way to artistic liberation, where blocks are dissolved, and where the artist's spirit soars free. So, venture forth into the dreamscapes, embrace the power within, and let your creativity soar to new heights.

REALIZING ARTISTIC PROJECTS IN WAKING LIFE

While the realm of lucid dreaming offers immense creative potential, it is equally important for artists to bring their artistic visions to life in the waking world. This section explores strategies and approaches for realizing artistic projects outside of dreamscapes, empowering artists to bridge the gap between their lucid dream experiences and their waking artistic practice. By channeling the inspiration, insights, and creativity gained from lucid dreaming, artists can manifest their artistic projects and share their unique expressions with the world.

- **Capturing Dreamscapes in Art:** Lucid dreams often present artists with vivid and fantastical dreamscapes that can serve as a wellspring of inspiration for their waking artistic projects. Artists can use various mediums such as painting, drawing, photography, or digital art to capture the essence of these dreamscapes and translate them into tangible artworks. By harnessing their skills and techniques, artists can recreate the dreamscapes' atmosphere, colors, textures, and emotions, offering viewers a glimpse into the magical realms they explored during their lucid dream experiences.

- **Translating Symbolism into Artistic Language:** Dreams are rich in symbolism, and artists can utilize this symbolic language to infuse their waking artistic projects with deeper meaning and layers of interpretation. By reflecting on the symbols and metaphors encountered within their lucid dreams, artists can identify recurring motifs, archetypes, or themes that resonate with their creative vision. They can then incorporate these symbols into their artwork, allowing viewers to engage with their personal journey, emotions, or universal human experiences through the visual language of symbolism.
- **Experimenting with New Techniques and Mediums:** Lucid dreaming serves as a fertile ground for artistic experimentation, and artists can carry this spirit of exploration

into their waking artistic practice. Inspired by their lucid dream experiences, artists can venture into uncharted territories by experimenting with new techniques, mediums, or artistic processes. This experimentation fuels creativity, fosters growth, and expands artistic horizons, allowing artists to push the boundaries of their craft and discover innovative ways to express their artistic vision.

- **Integrating Dream Characters into Artworks**: Dream characters encountered within lucid dreams can become muses and collaborators within the waking artistic practice. Artists can draw inspiration from the personalities, stories, or interactions with dream characters and integrate them into their artworks. This integration can take the form of incorporating dream characters' visual representations, capturing their essence through portraits, or even creating narratives or series of artworks inspired by the dream characters' presence. By weaving the dream characters' energy and presence into their artistic projects, artists infuse their creations with a touch of magic and a connection to the dreamscapes.
- **Seeking Collaborative Opportunities:** Lucid dreaming opens the doors to

collaborative possibilities, and artists can extend this spirit of collaboration into their waking artistic practice. Artists can seek collaborations with other artists, writers, musicians, or performers who share their passion for lucid dreaming or resonate with the themes explored within their dream experiences. By joining forces, artists can combine their creative talents and perspectives, creating multidisciplinary projects that merge different art forms and result in unique and immersive artistic experiences for the audience.

- **Sharing Lucid Dream Experiences through Art:** Lucid dreaming is a deeply personal and transformative experience, and artists can choose to share their lucid dream adventures through their artistic creations. Whether it be through visual art, poetry, literature, or performance, artists can capture the essence of their lucid dream experiences and invite others to glimpse the awe, wonder, and introspection that comes with lucid dreaming. Sharing these experiences through art not only spreads awareness about lucid dreaming but also invites viewers to contemplate their own dreams, consciousness, and the limitless creative potential that lies within.

- **Documenting and Reflecting on the Creative Journey:** As artists embark on their artistic projects inspired by lucid dreaming, it is essential to document their creative journey and reflect on the process. Artists can maintain a visual journal, a written diary, or a blog where they chronicle their artistic progress, challenges, breakthroughs, and insights gained from their lucid dream experiences. This documentation and reflection serve as a valuable resource, providing artists with a roadmap to navigate future artistic endeavors and allowing them to refine their artistic vision and voice over time.
- **Exhibiting and Showcasing Lucid Dream-inspired Art:** Once the artistic projects inspired by lucid dreaming are realized, it is important for artists to share their creations with the world. Artists can seek opportunities to exhibit their artwork in galleries, participate in group shows or art fairs, or even organize solo exhibitions that center around the theme of lucid dreaming. Through these exhibitions, artists not only showcase their artistic skills but also raise awareness about lucid dreaming as a source of inspiration and transformation.

- **Inspiring Others through Artistic Expression:** Artists who have experienced the profound impact of lucid dreaming can inspire others to explore their own creative potential through their artistic expression. By sharing their lucid dream-inspired artworks, artists can ignite curiosity, spark conversations, and encourage individuals to delve into the realm of lucid dreaming. Through their art, artists can become ambassadors for the power of dreams, consciousness, and self-discovery, inspiring others to embark on their own artistic and lucid dreaming journeys.
- **Continuing the Cycle of Inspiration:** Lucid dreaming is a continuous journey of exploration and inspiration. As artists realize their artistic projects within waking life, they simultaneously nourish their creative spirit, paving the way for new lucid dream experiences and artistic visions. By immersing themselves in the cycle of creation, reflection, and exploration, artists create a perpetual source of inspiration that fuels their artistic practice and keeps their connection to the dreamscapes alive.

Realizing artistic projects in waking life is a natural extension of the transformative power of lucid dreaming. By capturing dreamscapes, translating symbolism, experimenting with new techniques, integrating dream characters, seeking collaborations, sharing lucid dream experiences, documenting the creative journey, exhibiting artwork, inspiring others, and continuing the cycle of inspiration, artists bridge the gap between the dream world and the waking world, infusing their artistic practice with the magic, wisdom, and boundless creativity of lucid dreaming. It is through this integration of dreams and art that artists create meaningful connections, provoke emotions, and contribute to the ever-evolving landscape of artistic expression. So, let your artistic visions take flight, embrace the possibilities, and bring your lucid dream-inspired creations into the world.

SHARING THE DREAM: ART INSPIRED BY LUCID DREAMS

Lucid dreaming is not only a personal journey of exploration and self-discovery but also a wellspring of inspiration for artists across various creative disciplines. This section delves into the diverse forms of art inspired by lucid dreams and explores how artists use their unique mediums and artistic voices to convey the ethereal, transformative, and awe-inspiring experiences of lucid dreaming. From visual art to literature, music to film, artists have found ways to capture the essence of lucid dreaming and share it with audiences, inviting them into the mystical realm of dreams.

- **Visual Art:** Visual artists have long been captivated by the ethereal beauty and surreal imagery found within lucid dreams. Painters, illustrators, sculptors, and mixed media artists translate their dreamscapes and dream characters into captivating artworks. They use vibrant colors, intricate details, and imaginative compositions to recreate the otherworldly landscapes and entities encountered within their lucid dream experiences. Through their visual art, they offer viewers a glimpse into the magical and elusive realm of dreams, blurring the boundaries between fantasy and reality.
- **Surrealism and Fantasy Art:** Lucid dreaming and the artistic movement of surrealism share a profound connection. Surrealist artists, such as Salvador Dalí and René Magritte, were deeply influenced by the dream world and explored the subconscious mind through their artworks. Inspired by the dream-like quality of lucid dreams, surrealists sought to challenge conventional reality, juxtaposing

unlikely elements and creating enigmatic compositions. Similarly, contemporary fantasy artists draw from the rich symbolism and fantastical elements present in lucid dreams to create mesmerizing and enchanting artworks that transport viewers into realms of imagination and wonder.

- **Digital Art and Virtual Reality:** In the digital age, artists have embraced technology to bring their lucid dream-inspired visions to life. Digital artists utilize software, digital painting techniques, and 3D modeling to create immersive and interactive artworks that simulate the dreamscapes they have encountered. Virtual reality (VR) technology has opened up new possibilities for artists to create immersive experiences, allowing viewers to step into the lucid dream-inspired worlds and explore them firsthand. Through digital art and VR, artists bridge the gap between the physical and the imagined, offering viewers an unparalleled journey into the depths of their lucid dream experiences.
- **Literary Works:** Writers and poets have long sought inspiration from dreams and the subconscious mind. Lucid dreaming provides writers with a unique

lens through which they can explore the boundaries of reality, consciousness, and human experience. Authors like J.R.R. Tolkien, Haruki Murakami, and Neil Gaiman have incorporated elements of lucid dreaming into their novels, crafting intricate dreamscapes, and blurring the lines between waking and dreaming. Poets weave words into ethereal verses that capture the ephemeral nature of dreams and the profound insights gained from lucid dreaming. Through their literary works, writers transport readers into the realm of dreams, inviting them to question the nature of reality and explore the depths of the human psyche.

- **Music and Soundscapes:** Music has the power to evoke emotions, transport listeners to different worlds, and create ethereal experiences. Musicians and composers draw inspiration from the ethereal quality of lucid dreams to compose enchanting melodies, hypnotic rhythms, and atmospheric soundscapes. Ambient, electronic, and experimental music genres often explore dream-like states and incorporate elements of lucid dreaming, creating sonic tapestries that mirror the fluidity and enchantment of dreams. By crafting immersive soundscapes, musicians invite listeners to embark on their own sonic journeys, where reality and dreams merge.

- **Film and Animation:** The cinematic medium provides a visually compelling way to portray the enigmatic nature of lucid dreams. Filmmakers and animators use visual effects, surreal imagery, and nonlinear storytelling techniques to capture the essence of lucid dreaming on the screen. Films such as "Inception" and "Waking Life" explore the labyrinthine landscapes of dreams and the blurring of dream and reality. Through their visual storytelling, filmmakers create immersive experiences that challenge the viewers' perception and invite them to question the nature of their own reality.
- **Performance Art and Dance:** Performance artists and dancers harness the fluidity and boundless possibilities of lucid dreams to create captivating and transformative live experiences. They draw inspiration from the sensations, movements, and emotions experienced within lucid dreams, translating them into choreography, improvisation, or immersive performance installations. Through their physicality

and presence, performers invite audiences to explore the realms of the subconscious, bridging the gap between the tangible and the intangible.

- **Multidisciplinary Collaborations:** Lucid dreaming has also sparked collaborations between artists from different disciplines, resulting in unique multidisciplinary projects that combine visual art, music, dance, and more. These collaborations aim to create holistic artistic experiences that encompass the multifaceted aspects of lucid dreaming. By merging different art forms, artists push the boundaries of creativity and invite audiences to engage with the mystical world of dreams through a multi-sensory journey.
- **Artistic Exhibitions and Installations:** Exhibitions and installations centered around lucid dreaming provide a platform for artists to showcase their dream-inspired artworks collectively. These curated experiences immerse viewers in a dreamscape-like environment, blurring the boundaries between art and reality. Visitors are invited to explore the exhibited artworks, participate in interactive installations, and engage in dialogue about the intersection of art and lucid dreaming.

Through these exhibitions, artists create a shared space where the elusive and transformative nature of lucid dreaming can be experienced collectively.

- **Inspiring Creativity and Self-Reflection:** Lucid dream-inspired art not only provides aesthetic pleasure but also acts as a catalyst for introspection, contemplation, and self-reflection. By engaging with lucid dream-inspired artworks, viewers are prompted to explore their own dreams, consciousness, and creative potential. The evocative imagery, symbolism, and themes found within these artworks invite viewers to delve into the depths of their own subconscious and contemplate the nature of reality, perception, and the interconnectedness of the human experience.

Art inspired by lucid dreams holds the power to transport audiences into the realms of the subconscious, to question the boundaries of reality, and to ignite the flame of creativity and imagination. Through visual art, literature, music, film, performance, and multidisciplinary collaborations, artists create bridges between the intangible world of dreams and the tangible world of artistic expression. By sharing their lucid dream-inspired creations, artists invite viewers to embark on their own journeys of self-discovery, expansion, and awe-inspiring wonder. So, step into the realm of lucid dream-inspired art, and let your imagination take flight.

CONCLUSION

Lucid dreaming holds immense potential for unlocking creativity and artistic expression. By tapping into the vast reservoir of the dream world, artists can transcend the limitations of reality, ignite their imagination, and bring their wildest dreams to life. Through lucid dreaming, the artist's journey becomes an ever-evolving exploration of the boundless possibilities of the creative mind. Embrace the power of lucid dreaming and allow it to guide you on a transformative artistic odyssey that knows no bounds. The dream world awaits, ready to reveal its secrets and inspire your greatest artistic achievements.

CHAPTER 9

Healing and Self-Discovery

INTRODUCTION

In this chapter, we embark on an extraordinary journey of healing and self-discovery through the realm of lucid dreaming. Imagine a world where you have the power to explore the depths of your subconscious mind, confront emotional wounds, and unlock the doors to profound personal growth. Lucid dreaming offers a remarkable platform for therapeutic exploration, providing a safe and immersive environment where we can engage with our inner landscapes in transformative ways.

Within the realm of lucid dreaming, we gain conscious awareness while dreaming, enabling us to actively participate in and shape our dream experiences. This unique state of consciousness allows us to tap into the vast potential of our subconscious, uncover hidden insights, and embark on a profound journey of healing and self-discovery. Lucid dreaming serves as a gateway to our inner worlds, where the limitations of physical reality dissolve and the mind is free to explore uncharted territories.

One of the remarkable aspects of lucid dreaming is its ability to facilitate emotional healing. Dreams often serve as a conduit for processing and releasing emotions, and when we enter a lucid dream, we gain the power to engage with our emotions in a conscious and deliberate manner. Through lucid dreaming, we can confront and address emotional traumas, phobias, and anxieties, providing a safe space for exploration, resolution, and integration.

Lucid dreaming can be a valuable tool for addressing phobias and anxiety disorders. By intentionally inducing lucidity during a dream where fears are present, we can gradually expose ourselves to fear-inducing scenarios while maintaining a sense of control and safety. This process, known as desensitization, allows us to confront and overcome our fears within the dream world, ultimately leading to a reduction of anxiety and an increased sense of empowerment in waking life.

Moreover, lucid dreaming holds tremendous potential for healing traumatic experiences. Within the lucid dream state, we can revisit and engage with traumatic events, offering an opportunity for processing, releasing, and reframing our past traumas. By consciously navigating these experiences, we can gain new insights, rewire negative associations, and initiate profound healing and transformation.

The realm of lucid dreaming also provides a nurturing environment for emotional integration and resolution. In a lucid dream, we can engage in dialogue with dream characters, aspects of ourselves, and even personifications of our emotions. Through these interactions, we gain a deeper understanding of our emotions, reconcile inner conflicts, and foster emotional harmony within ourselves. The conscious exploration of emotions within the dream state allows us to engage with them in a supportive and transformative way.

Beyond its therapeutic potential, lucid dreaming opens the door to self-exploration and personal growth. Within the vast expanse of our dreamscapes, we can access the depths of our subconscious mind, unveiling hidden potentials, talents, and creativity. Lucid dreams offer a playground for experimentation, allowing us to try new skills, engage in imaginary scenarios, and tap into untapped aspects of ourselves.

Through lucid dreaming, we can also explore past lives and parallel realities, expanding our understanding of ourselves beyond the limitations of our current existence. Lucid dreams can provide glimpses into alternative versions of ourselves, shedding light on our interconnectedness and the infinite possibilities that exist within the fabric of consciousness.

Moreover, lucid dreams allow us to connect with our inner wisdom and higher selves. Within the dream state, we can engage in dialogue with dream characters that represent aspects of ourselves or embody wisdom and guidance. These interactions can provide us with profound insights, clarity, and intuitive guidance that can be carried forward into our waking lives.

Cultivating resilience and overcoming limiting beliefs is another area where lucid dreaming can be transformative. By consciously challenging and transforming limiting beliefs within the dream state, we can build resilience, foster a growth mindset, and empower ourselves to break free from self-imposed limitations. Lucid dreaming becomes a playground for self-empowerment, where we can design empowering dream scenarios and experiences that strengthen our sense of self and expand our perceived boundaries.

In the following sections of this chapter, we will explore various techniques and practices for utilizing lucid dreaming as a tool for healing and self-discovery. We will delve into the process of emotional healing within lucid dreams, address specific techniques for self-exploration and personal growth, and examine the integration of lucid dream insights into waking life. Prepare to embark on a profound journey of self-exploration and transformation as we harness the extraordinary power of lucid dreaming for healing and self-discovery.

LUCID DREAMING AS A THERAPEUTIC TOOL

1. Understanding Emotional Healing in Lucid Dreams

Lucid dreaming serves as a remarkable tool for emotional healing, providing a unique platform for the processing and release of emotions. Within the lucid dream state, we gain conscious awareness of our emotions, allowing us to engage with them in a deliberate and transformative manner.

When we enter a lucid dream, we can intentionally direct our focus towards the emotions that arise within the dream. By acknowledging and embracing these emotions, we create an opportunity for healing and resolution. The lucid dream environment offers a safe space for emotional exploration, free from the constraints and judgments of the waking world.

One of the ways lucid dreaming facilitates emotional healing is through the direct confrontation and resolution of emotional traumas. Within the lucid dream state, we can revisit past traumatic experiences, engaging with them in a controlled and empowered manner. This process allows us to reframe our perception of the trauma, gain new insights, and initiate healing and transformation.

In lucid dreams, we can also engage in dialogue with dream characters or symbolic representations of our emotions. These interactions provide a profound opportunity to gain a deeper understanding of our emotions, their origins, and their significance in our lives. Through conversations with these aspects of ourselves, we can uncover hidden layers of emotional wounds and work towards their resolution.

2. Addressing Phobias and Anxiety Disorders

Phobias and anxiety disorders can significantly impact our quality of life, limiting our experiences and causing distress. Lucid dreaming offers a powerful approach to addressing and overcoming these challenges by providing a controlled environment for exposure therapy and desensitization.

By inducing lucidity within a dream that contains elements of our phobias or triggers our anxiety, we can gradually expose ourselves to these fear-inducing stimuli. The lucid dream state allows us to approach these situations with a sense of control and safety, reducing the overwhelming nature of real-life encounters.

Through repeated exposure in lucid dreams, we can desensitize ourselves to our phobias or anxiety triggers, gradually reducing the fear response. As we gain confidence and mastery within the dream state, these positive experiences can translate into increased resilience and reduced anxiety in waking life.

Lucid dreaming also offers an opportunity to engage with phobias or anxiety triggers in imaginative and empowering ways. By reshaping the dream environment or altering the outcome of the dream scenario, we can transform the narrative and challenge the power of our fears. These empowered experiences within lucid dreams can foster a sense of empowerment and courage that can be carried into our daily lives.

3. Healing Traumatic Experiences

Traumatic experiences can leave deep emotional scars that affect our well-being and relationships. Lucid dreaming provides a unique avenue for healing these wounds, offering a safe and controlled space to revisit and reprocess traumatic events.

Within the lucid dream state, we can engage with traumatic memories and experiences in a deliberate and empowered manner. By consciously confronting the trauma within the dream, we can gain new perspectives, process unresolved emotions, and initiate the healing process.

One approach to healing trauma in lucid dreams is through gradual exposure and desensitization. By revisiting the traumatic event within the dream state, we can engage with it at a pace that feels comfortable and safe. This allows us to gradually integrate the traumatic experience and create a sense of closure and resolution.

In addition to exposure and desensitization, lucid dreaming offers opportunities for transformative experiences that reframe our perception of trauma. Within the dream, we can rewrite the narrative, explore alternative outcomes, and engage with supportive dream characters or aspects of ourselves that facilitate healing and resolution.

4. Emotional Integration and Resolution

Lucid dreaming provides a powerful platform for emotional integration and resolution. Within the dream state, we can engage in dialogue with dream characters, aspects of ourselves, and even personifications of our emotions. These interactions allow us to gain a deeper understanding of our emotions, reconcile inner conflicts, and foster emotional harmony.

By engaging with dream characters that represent different aspects of ourselves, we can explore and integrate various emotions and conflicting parts of our identity. This process of dialogue and integration within lucid dreams can lead to a greater sense of self-awareness, self-acceptance, and emotional balance.

In lucid dreams, we can also engage in symbolic activities or rituals that facilitate emotional healing and resolution. These activities may include visualization, guided imagery, or symbolic gestures that represent the release or transformation of emotions. By actively participating in these activities within the dream, we create a profound sense of closure and emotional resolution.

Moreover, lucid dreaming allows us to experiment with different emotional responses and perspectives. By consciously choosing how we interact with dream scenarios and dream characters, we can explore alternative emotional reactions and cultivate more empowering emotional patterns. This process of experimentation and exploration within lucid dreams can lead to a greater sense of emotional flexibility and resilience in waking life.

In the following sections of this chapter, we will further explore specific techniques and practices for utilizing lucid dreaming as a tool for emotional healing and self-discovery. We will delve into the methods of creating healing and empowering dreamscapes, the process of lucid dream incubation for specific healing intentions, and strategies for integrating lucid dream insights into our waking lives. Prepare to embark on a profound journey of emotional healing and self-discovery as we harness the transformative power of lucid dreaming.

TECHNIQUES FOR HEALING AND SELF-DISCOVERY IN LUCID DREAMS

1. Creating Healing and Empowering Dreamscapes

Creating healing and empowering dreamscapes is a powerful technique within lucid dreaming that allows us to design and manifest dream environments conducive to emotional healing and self-discovery. By consciously shaping the dream environment, we can create a nurturing space that supports our healing journey.

To begin, it is helpful to set a clear intention before entering the lucid dream state. This intention can be focused on emotional healing, personal growth, or any specific area of self-discovery you wish to explore. By setting a clear intention, you prime your subconscious mind to align with your desired outcomes within the dream.

Once lucid within the dream, take a moment to ground yourself and connect with your intention. This can be done through deep breathing, affirmations, or visualization techniques. As you cultivate a sense of presence and focus, you can begin to shape the dream environment to create a healing and empowering dreamscape.

One technique for creating healing dreamscapes is through visualization. Imagine a serene and safe environment that resonates with your emotional well-being. It could be a lush garden, a peaceful beach, or any setting that brings you a sense of comfort and tranquility. Visualize the details of the dream environment, engaging all your senses to make the experience as vivid and immersive as possible.

In addition to visualization, you can also incorporate healing elements into the dream environment. For example, you may envision a healing pool or a sacred temple within the dream where you can immerse yourself in transformative energies. These symbolic elements can serve as catalysts for emotional healing and self-discovery.

Furthermore, interacting with dream characters or dream guides can enhance the healing and self-discovery processes. Seek out supportive dream characters or create imaginary companions who embody qualities that align with your healing journey. Engage in conversations with these characters, seeking their guidance, wisdom, and support. These interactions can provide profound insights and facilitate emotional healing within the dream.

2. Lucid Dream Incubation for Specific Healing Intentions

Lucid dream incubation is a technique where you set a specific intention before falling asleep to enter a lucid dream focused on a particular area of healing or self-discovery. By programming your dreams, you can actively engage with specific issues, emotions, or aspects of yourself within the lucid dream state.

To begin, choose a specific healing intention that you wish to explore in a lucid dream. It could be related to emotional healing, releasing past traumas, finding clarity on a particular issue, or connecting with your inner wisdom. Write down your intention on a piece of paper or repeat it mentally before going to sleep, reinforcing your commitment to entering a lucid dream focused on this intention.

As you drift off to sleep, visualize yourself becoming lucid within the dream, fully aware of your intention. Imagine yourself engaging in the specific healing or self-discovery process you desire to explore. By anchoring your intention in your mind, you create a pathway for your subconscious to navigate towards this healing experience.

When you wake up from a dream during the night, take a moment to recall any details or emotions from the dream. If the dream is relevant to your healing intention, journal about it or reflect on its significance. This practice increases your dream recall and strengthens your connection with your healing journey.

Throughout the day, reinforce your intention through reality testing and mindfulness. Engage in regular reality checks, questioning your state of consciousness, and reinforcing the idea of becoming lucid in your dreams. This practice increases self-awareness and primes your mind for the possibility of entering a lucid dream focused on your healing intention.

During the night, consider incorporating techniques such as Wake-Back-to-Bed (WBTB) or Mnemonic-Induced Lucid Dreaming (MILD) to enhance your chances of becoming lucid and engaging with your healing intention. These techniques involve briefly waking up during the night and then returning to sleep with the focused intention of becoming lucid in a dream related to your healing journey.

Once you achieve lucidity within the dream, remind yourself of your healing intention. Engage with the dream environment and dream characters, seeking opportunities for healing, self-exploration, and emotional resolution. Embrace the experience with an open mind and heart, allowing the dream to guide you towards profound healing insights.

3. Integrating Lucid Dream Insights into Waking Life

The transformative power of lucid dreaming extends beyond the dream state itself. The insights and experiences gained in lucid dreams can be integrated into our waking lives, supporting our ongoing healing and self-discovery journey.

Upon waking from a lucid dream, take a moment to reflect on the emotions, symbols, and messages that emerged during the dream. Journaling about the dream experience can deepen your understanding and provide a record for future reference. Pay attention to any recurring themes or symbols that may hold significance for your healing process.

Once you have captured the essence of the lucid dream, explore ways to bring its insights and lessons into your waking life. Consider how the emotions experienced in the dream can be acknowledged and processed in your daily routines. Reflect on the symbols and imagery encountered in the dream, seeking connections and meanings that can be translated into actionable steps for personal growth.

Engage in creative outlets such as art, writing, or movement to express and integrate the emotions and insights gained from the lucid dream. Creating artwork inspired by the dream or writing a reflective piece can deepen your connection with its transformative energy. Allow your creative expression to become a bridge between the dream world and your waking reality.

Additionally, mindfulness practices can enhance the integration of lucid dream insights into daily life. Cultivate present-moment awareness and self-compassion, allowing yourself to fully embody the lessons and transformations experienced in the dream. By bringing conscious attention to your thoughts, emotions, and actions, you create space for the integration of your lucid dream wisdom.

Share your lucid dream experiences with supportive communities, friends, or therapists who can provide guidance and insights. Verbalizing your dream experiences allows for external processing and opens up opportunities for new perspectives and interpretations. Engaging in discussions about your dreams can deepen your understanding and solidify the integration of the insights gained.

Lastly, consider revisiting lucid dreams that hold particular significance for your healing and self-discovery journey. Through lucid dream reentry techniques such as Mnemonic-Induced Lucid Dreaming (MILD) or Wake-Initiated Lucid Dreaming (WILD), you can consciously return to a previous lucid dream and deepen your exploration of its transformative potential. This iterative process can lead to ongoing growth, healing, and self-discovery over time.

As you continue to integrate lucid dream insights into your waking life, remember to be patient and gentle with yourself. Healing and self-discovery are ongoing processes, and each lucid dream experience contributes to your personal journey of growth and transformation. Embrace the wisdom and guidance offered by lucid dreaming and allow it to positively impact your life beyond the boundaries of the dream state.

4. Emotional Journaling and Reflection

Emotional journaling and reflection are valuable practices for processing and integrating the emotions experienced in lucid dreams. By engaging in these practices, we deepen our understanding of the emotional landscapes within our dreams and gain insights into our inner world.

After waking from a lucid dream, take the time to write down your emotional experiences in a journal. Describe the intensity, quality, and nuances of the emotions you encountered. Explore any shifts or transformations in your emotional state throughout the dream. Allow yourself to freely express and explore the emotional tapestry woven within the dream.

As you write, reflect on the possible meanings and connections between the emotions in your lucid dream and your waking life. Consider any parallels or resonances between the emotions experienced in the dream and the emotions you are currently navigating in your everyday experiences. By drawing connections between dream and waking emotions, you gain deeper insights into your emotional patterns and triggers.

Journaling also provides an opportunity to explore the potential underlying messages or lessons encoded within the emotional landscape of the dream. Reflect on how the emotions experienced in the dream might relate to your personal growth, healing, or self-discovery. Seek understanding of the underlying emotional currents that the dream is bringing to your awareness.

In addition to emotional journaling, engage in reflective practices that allow you to explore the emotional content of your lucid dreams. Contemplative activities such as meditation, mindfulness, or simply sitting in quiet reflection can help you access and process the emotions experienced within the dream state.

During your reflection, notice any recurring emotional themes or patterns that emerge across multiple lucid dreams. These patterns can provide valuable insights into persistent emotional challenges or unresolved aspects of your psyche. By recognizing these patterns, you can begin to consciously work on healing and integrating the underlying emotional issues.

5. Emotional Release and Integration Practices

Emotional release and integration practices within the context of lucid dreaming allow us to consciously engage with and process challenging emotions, facilitating healing and self-discovery. These practices provide a safe and controlled environment for emotional exploration and release.

One technique for emotional release in lucid dreams is through visualization and symbolic gestures.

Within the dream, visualize the emotions you wish to release taking the form of energy or symbols. As you engage with these representations, imagine physically releasing or transforming them. For example, you may envision yourself throwing them into a fire, letting them dissolve into light, or watching them drift away on a breeze. This symbolic act of release can be accompanied by a sense of catharsis and emotional liberation.

Another approach to emotional release in lucid dreams is through expressive movement, or cathartic release. Within the dream, engage in physical movement that reflects the emotions you wish to release. Dance, scream, cry, or engage in any form of physical expression that allows you to embody and release the emotional energy held within. By consciously moving and expressing emotions within the dream state, you create a pathway for their release and integration.

Lucid dreams also provide opportunities for inner dialogue and self-compassion, facilitating emotional integration. Engage in conversations with dream characters or aspects of yourself that represent different emotions or parts of your psyche. Offer empathy and understanding to these aspects, allowing for the integration and healing of fragmented emotions. By cultivating self-compassion within the dream, you foster emotional integration and inner harmony.

Engaging in self-care practices within the lucid dream state can further support emotional release and integration. Create dream scenarios that promote nurturing and self-soothing activities. For example, you may choose to immerse yourself in a warm and healing bath, receive a massage, or engage in activities that bring you joy and comfort. By consciously engaging in self-care within the dream, you reinforce the importance of emotional well-being and self-nurturing in your waking life.

As you engage in emotional release and integration practices within lucid dreams, remember to approach them with gentleness and self-compassion. Allow yourself to navigate the emotions at your own pace and comfort level. The goal is to create a space for emotional exploration, healing, and integration, promoting a greater sense of emotional well-being and self-discovery.

By utilizing these techniques for healing and self-discovery within lucid dreams, we unlock a profound potential for emotional growth and transformation. The lucid dream state becomes a sacred space where we can explore, process, and integrate our emotions, leading to a greater sense of emotional harmony, self-awareness, and personal empowerment. Embrace the power of lucid dreaming as a catalyst for emotional healing and self-discovery, and embark on a transformative journey within the depths of your own mind.

TECHNIQUES FOR SELF-IMPROVEMENT AND PERSONAL GROWTH IN LUCID DREAMS

1. Skill Development and Enhancement

Lucid dreams offer a unique platform for skill development and enhancement, allowing us to practice and improve various abilities within the safe confines of the dream world. By engaging in targeted skill-building exercises during lucid dreams, we can accelerate our learning curve and cultivate mastery in different areas of interest.

To begin, select a specific skill or ability that you wish to develop or improve. It can be anything from playing a musical instrument to speaking a foreign language or honing a physical activity like martial arts. Choose a skill that resonates with your personal goals and aspirations, as this will enhance your motivation and focus within the lucid dream.

Before entering the dream state, take some time to visualize yourself skillfully performing the chosen activity. Imagine the precise movements, sounds, and sensations associated with the skill. By vividly envisioning yourself engaging in the desired skill, you prime your mind for the upcoming practice within the lucid dream.

Once lucid within the dream, affirm your intention to engage in skill development and enhancement. Seek out an appropriate environment or setting that supports the practice of your chosen skill. For example, if you want to improve your tennis serve, imagine yourself on a tennis court with all the necessary equipment.

Engage in deliberate and focused practice within the lucid dream. Pay close attention to the nuances of the skill, such as form, timing, and coordination. Experiment, make adjustments, and receive feedback from the dream environment. Remember that the dream world can offer a heightened sense of perception and responsiveness, allowing for accelerated learning and skill acquisition.

It can be beneficial to incorporate visualization techniques into the dream. Imagine yourself successfully executing the skill with precision and ease. Visualize the desired outcome and the satisfaction that comes with mastery. This mental rehearsal within the dream reinforces neural pathways associated with the skill, contributing to its development and enhancement.

Upon waking from the lucid dream, take a few moments to reflect on the experience. Journal about any insights, breakthroughs, or challenges encountered during the practice. This reflection enhances the integration of the dream experience into your waking life, supporting further skill development and growth.

2. Problem Solving and Creativity Boost

Lucid dreaming provides fertile ground for problem-solving and creative exploration. Within the dream state, the constraints and limitations of the waking world can be transcended, allowing for unconventional insights and innovative solutions to emerge. By harnessing the power of lucid dreaming, we can tap into our creative potential and effectively address complex challenges.

To leverage lucid dreams for problem-solving and creativity, start by clearly defining the issue or challenge you wish to address. It could be a personal problem, a creative block, or a decision you need to make. Write down or mentally articulate the problem before falling asleep, affirming your intention to gain insights and find solutions within the lucid dream state.

As you enter the lucid dream, bring the problem or challenge to the forefront of your awareness. Embrace a curious and open mindset, allowing the dream to unfold and providing fresh perspectives and ideas. Be receptive to the symbolism, metaphors, and unexpected connections that may arise within the dream, as these can offer valuable insights for problem-solving and creativity.

Engage in active exploration and experimentation within the dream. Seek out dream characters or dream guides who can offer guidance and wisdom related to the problem or challenge at hand. Engage in conversations, ask questions, and listen attentively to the responses. The dream characters may embody different perspectives or aspects of your psyche, providing diverse insights and alternative viewpoints.

Experiment with different approaches and solutions within the lucid dream. Test out unconventional ideas, break free from traditional thinking patterns, and explore the boundaries of what is possible. The dream state is a realm of limitless imagination and creativity, allowing you to push the boundaries of your problem-solving and creative capabilities.

When you awaken, take the time to reflect on the insights and ideas generated in the lucid dream. Journal about the symbols, connections, and solutions that emerged. Look for patterns or recurring themes that may offer deeper meaning and relevance to your waking life. Consider how the dream insights can be applied to the problem or challenge you are facing.

It's important to note that while lucid dreams can provide valuable insights and creative breakthroughs, it's essential to validate and test these ideas in the waking world. Implement the solutions or ideas that resonate with you and evaluate their effectiveness. By combining the imaginative power of lucid dreaming with real-world application, you can harness the full potential of problem-solving and creativity.

3. Personal Transformation and Self-Actualization

Lucid dreaming serves as a gateway to personal transformation and self-actualization, allowing us to explore and cultivate our highest potential. Within the lucid dream state, we can consciously engage with our subconscious mind, identify limiting beliefs, and initiate profound inner changes.

To embark on a journey of personal transformation within lucid dreams, start by setting clear intentions for the qualities or aspects of yourself that you wish to develop or embody. It could be qualities such as courage, compassion, self-confidence, or resilience. Affirm your intention to cultivate these qualities within the dream state and allow the lucid dreams to become a training ground for personal growth.

Upon becoming lucid in a dream, connect with your intention for personal transformation. Engage with dream characters or dream guides that embody the qualities or wisdom you seek. Engage in conversations, observe their behavior, and learn from their embodiment of the qualities you aspire to cultivate within yourself.

Within the lucid dream, actively practice and embody the desired qualities. Engage in scenarios or situations that challenge you to demonstrate courage, compassion, or other qualities you wish to develop. Consciously respond to dream events with the intention of expressing and strengthening these qualities. Embrace the opportunities for growth and transformation that the dream presents.

Visualization techniques can be particularly powerful within lucid dreams for personal transformation.

Imagine yourself fully embodying the desired qualities, visualizing how it feels, looks, and sounds. See yourself acting, speaking, and responding from a place of self-actualization. By vividly envisioning your transformed self within the dream, you reinforce positive neural patterns and create a blueprint for personal growth.

Upon awakening, take the time to reflect on the experiences and insights gained during the lucid dream. Journal about the lessons learned, the challenges faced, and the progress made. Consider how these insights can be applied to your waking life and initiate practical steps to integrate the qualities and transformations into your everyday experiences.

It's important to approach personal transformation within lucid dreams with patience, self-compassion, and a growth mindset. Remember that personal growth is an ongoing process, and each lucid dream experience contributes to your journey of self-actualization. Embrace the opportunities for self-discovery and transformation that lucid dreaming offers, and actively cultivate your highest potential within the depths of your dreams.

In conclusion, lucid dreaming provides a profound platform for self-improvement, personal growth, and transformation. By harnessing the power of lucidity, we can engage in skill development, problem-solving, and creativity, as well as embark on a journey of personal transformation and self-actualization. Embrace the potential of lucid dreaming as a tool for unlocking your inner capabilities, expanding your consciousness, and enhancing your overall well-being.

4. Manifesting and Goal Achievement

Lucid dreaming offers a unique opportunity to harness the power of the subconscious mind to manifest and achieve your goals. Within the lucid dream state, you can actively engage in the processes of visualization, intention setting, and manifestation, accelerating your progress towards your desired outcomes.

To begin, clearly define the goals or desires you wish to manifest within the lucid dream. It can be anything from personal aspirations, career goals, or even experiences you want to have. Write them down or hold them in your mind with clarity and specificity before entering the dream state.

Once lucid within the dream, remind yourself of your intentions and the goals you want to manifest. Visualize yourself already having achieved the desired outcomes. Immerse yourself fully in the experience, engaging all your senses to create a vivid and immersive dream reality. By vividly envisioning the desired manifestations, you activate the power of the subconscious mind to work towards their realization.

As you explore your dream world, actively seek out opportunities and experiences that align with your goals. Engage with dream characters, dream environments, or symbolic representations that reflect the desired outcomes. Interact with them, learn from them, and allow them to guide you towards the manifestation of your goals.

During the lucid dream, you can also experiment with techniques such as affirmations and visualization exercises. Repeatedly affirm positive statements related to your goals, such as "I am confident and successful" or "I attract abundance and opportunities." Visualize the desired outcomes in detail, incorporating the emotions and sensations associated with achieving them. By consistently reinforcing these positive beliefs and images within the dream, you strengthen the manifestation process.

Upon awakening, reflect on the experiences and insights gained during the lucid dream. Journal about the manifestations and any synchronicities or signs that appeared within the dream. Look for connections between your dream experiences and your waking life, as these can offer guidance and inspiration for taking action towards your goals. Take note of any inspired ideas or intuitive nudges that arise from the dream state.

It's important to remember that while lucid dreaming can be a powerful tool for manifestation, it should be complemented by action in the waking world. Use the insights and inspiration gained from the lucid dream to inform your actions and decision-making in your daily life. Take practical steps towards your goals and remain open to the opportunities and synchronicities that present themselves.

3.5 Transcendence and Spiritual Exploration

Lucid dreaming has long been regarded as a pathway to transcendent and spiritual experiences. Within the lucid dream state, we can explore the depths of our consciousness, connect with higher states of awareness, and access profound spiritual insights and wisdom.

To engage in spiritual exploration within lucid dreams, cultivate a mindset of openness and receptivity. Set the intention to connect with your higher self, the collective unconscious, or the divine source of wisdom and guidance. Affirm your willingness to receive spiritual insights and to explore the mysteries of existence.

Once lucid within the dream, practice mindfulness and present moment awareness. Engage in meditative practices, observing the thoughts, sensations, and emotions that arise within the dream. Notice the inherent beauty and profound nature of the dream experience. By cultivating a state of presence and mindfulness within the lucid dream, you open yourself to spiritual revelations and experiences.

Within the lucid dream, seek out dream characters or dream guides that embody spiritual wisdom and guidance. Engage in conversations, ask questions, and listen attentively to their responses. These dream characters may serve as symbolic representations of higher aspects of your consciousness or external manifestations of spiritual guides. Embrace the teachings and insights they offer, allowing them to deepen your spiritual exploration.

Engaging in practices such as prayer, contemplation, or energy work within a lucid dream can further enhance spiritual experiences. Connect with the divine or higher power through prayer, expressing gratitude, or seeking guidance. Consider profound questions about the nature of existence, the meaning of life, or your spiritual purpose. Engage in energy work, such as visualizing healing or sending love and light to yourself and others.

Upon awakening from the lucid dream, take time to reflect on the spiritual insights and experiences. Journal about the wisdom received, the lessons learned, and the emotions felt during the dream. Look for ways to integrate these spiritual insights into your waking life. Explore spiritual practices such as meditation, mindfulness, or contemplation that can further deepen your spiritual journey.

It's important to approach spiritual exploration within lucid dreams with humility, respect, and an open mind. Understand that the nature of spirituality is deeply personal and can vary greatly from person to person. Embrace the diversity of spiritual experiences that may arise within the lucid dream state and allow them to contribute to your overall spiritual growth and understanding.

In conclusion, lucid dreaming provides a powerful platform for self-improvement, personal growth, and spiritual exploration. By engaging in skill development, problem-solving, personal transformation, manifestation, and spiritual practices within lucid dreams, we unlock new dimensions of our consciousness and expand our understanding of ourselves and the world. Embrace the potential of lucid dreaming as a tool for holistic growth and embark on a journey of self-discovery, empowerment, and spiritual awakening within the realm of your dreams.

CONCLUSION

In conclusion, lucid dreaming is a remarkable tool that opens up a world of possibilities for self-improvement, personal growth, and self-discovery. Throughout this chapter, we have explored the various ways in which lucid dreaming can be utilized to enhance our lives and tap into our full potential.

We began by delving into the realm of personal growth and self-improvement, where we discovered how lucid dreaming can serve as a platform for skill development, problem-solving, creativity, and personal transformation. By consciously engaging with our dreams, we can accelerate our learning, overcome obstacles, unlock our creative potential, and cultivate the qualities and traits we aspire to embody.

We then ventured into the realm of manifestation and goal achievement, where we explored how lucid dreaming can be harnessed to manifest our desires and accelerate our progress towards our goals. Through visualization, intention setting, and immersive dream experiences, we can leverage the power of our subconscious mind to manifest the life we envision for ourselves.

The exploration of spirituality and transcendence within lucid dreams revealed the profound depth and potential for spiritual growth and enlightenment. By connecting with our higher selves, seeking spiritual guidance, and engaging in meditative practices within the dream state, we can gain insights into the mysteries of existence and deepen our connection to the divine.

It is important to emphasize that the true power of lucid dreaming lies not only in the experiences within the dream state but also in their integration into our waking lives. The insights, lessons, and breakthroughs gained from lucid dreams can have a transformative impact when applied in practical ways to our daily lives. Journaling, reflecting, and actively implementing the lessons learned can foster lasting changes and propel us forward on our path of personal evolution.

Throughout this chapter, we have provided numerous techniques, exercises, and strategies to help you navigate the realm of lucid dreaming and harness its potential for growth and self-discovery. Remember that lucid dreaming is a skill that requires practice, patience, and dedication. The more you engage in these practices, the more proficient and insightful you will become in the realm of lucid dreams.

As you embark on your own lucid dreaming journey, we encourage you to approach it with an open mind, a spirit of curiosity, and a sense of wonder. Embrace the possibilities that await you in the realm of lucid dreams and allow them to guide you towards greater self-awareness, personal growth, and spiritual awakening.

Now is the time to take action. Commit to developing your lucid dreaming skills, explore the techniques that resonate with you, and create a regular practice that supports your growth and exploration. Keep a dream journal, engage in reality testing, and immerse yourself in the incredible experiences that lucid dreaming has to offer.

Remember that lucid dreaming is not only a tool for personal growth and self-discovery but also a gateway to extraordinary adventures and profound insights. It is a realm where the boundaries of reality dissolve, where imagination takes flight, and where the depths of your consciousness are waiting to be explored.

So, dear reader, we invite you to step into the world of lucid dreaming with confidence and excitement. Embrace the transformative potential it holds, and allow your dreams to become a portal to a more vibrant, fulfilling, and awakened life.

Dream boldly, explore fearlessly, and may your lucid dreaming journey be filled with wonder, wisdom, and infinite possibilities.

CHAPTER 10

Lucid Dreaming and Mindfulness

INTRODUCTION

Welcome to Chapter 10 of "The Power of Lucid Dreaming." In this final chapter, we embark on a profound exploration of the fascinating intersection between lucid dreaming and mindfulness. Lucid dreaming, the state of being aware and conscious within a dream, offers incredible opportunities for self-discovery, creativity, and personal growth. Mindfulness, on the other hand, is the practice of being fully present and aware in the current moment, cultivating a non-judgmental attitude towards our thoughts, emotions, and sensations. When these two transformative practices merge, a world of limitless possibilities emerges.

Throughout this book, we have delved into the realms of lucid dreaming, exploring its definition, history, and scientific foundations. We have discovered techniques for inducing and controlling lucid dreams, empowering readers to unlock the gateway to conscious dream exploration. We have also explored the power of lucid dreaming for creative expression, healing, and self-discovery. Now, in this final chapter, we dive deeper into the profound connection between lucid dreaming and mindfulness.

Mindfulness, as a practice, has gained immense popularity in recent years for its ability to bring clarity, peace, and a sense of connectedness to our waking lives. By cultivating mindful awareness, we become more attuned to the present moment, fostering a deeper understanding of ourselves and the world around us. Mindfulness allows us to observe our thoughts, emotions, and sensations without judgment, creating a space for acceptance and self-compassion.

The connection between lucid dreaming and mindfulness may not be immediately apparent, but as we delve into the intricacies of these practices, we discover the harmonious dance they engage in. Both lucid dreaming and mindfulness involve cultivating awareness and exploring the depths of consciousness. Both offer pathways to transcend our ordinary state of being and tap into the infinite realms of the mind.

Lucid dreaming can be seen as an extension of mindfulness into the dream state. When we become lucid within a dream, we bring a state of heightened awareness and mindfulness into the realm of imagination. We step into a world where our thoughts manifest instantly and where we can navigate and explore the vast landscapes of our dreamscape with intention and curiosity. In this state of lucidity, we can apply the principles of mindfulness, observing our dream experiences without judgment and fully engaging with the present moment.

Practicing mindfulness during our waking lives lays a solid foundation for lucid dreaming. By cultivating present-moment awareness and non-reactivity in our everyday experiences, we enhance our self-reflective capacities. Mindfulness allows us to become more attuned to the subtle cues and patterns within our waking experiences, creating a heightened sense of self-awareness. This increased awareness can then carry over into our dream lives, creating fertile ground for lucid dreaming to flourish.

In this chapter, we explore various techniques for combining lucid dreaming and mindfulness. We delve into the art of setting intentions for mindful lucidity, affirming our desire to be present, aware, and engaged within our dreams. We discover how reality testing, a technique commonly used to induce lucid dreams, can be enhanced by incorporating mindful awareness. By approaching reality tests with a sense of curiosity and non-judgment, we cultivate a mindful attitude towards our experiences, increasing our chances of recognizing the dream state.

Once we achieve lucidity within a dream, we can deepen the experience by engaging in mindful reality checks. By employing mindful awareness, we can explore the dream environment with a non-reactive and curious attitude. We can examine dream objects, observe sensory details, and question the nature of our perceptions. This mindful approach enhances the vividness of the lucid dream and allows for deeper self-reflection and exploration within the dream state.

Furthermore, lucid dreams provide a unique platform for practicing meditation and other mindfulness techniques. We can engage in various meditation practices, such as breath awareness, body scanning, and loving-kindness meditation, while lucid dreaming. By integrating these practices into our lucid dreams, we can deepen our connection to the present moment, expand our awareness, and cultivate a sense of inner peace and stillness within the dream state.

The synergy between lucid dreaming and mindfulness offers profound benefits for personal growth and self-discovery. By combining these practices, we can deepen our self-awareness, transform emotional patterns, and access profound spiritual experiences. Lucid dreaming provides a safe and immersive environment for exploring aspects of ourselves that may be hidden or repressed, leading to increased self-awareness and personal integration. Mindful awareness allows us to approach challenging emotions and experiences within the dream state with compassion, fostering healing and emotional transformation.

In conclusion, as we embark on this journey of lucid dreaming and mindfulness, let us set clear intentions, engage in reality testing with mindful awareness, and explore various mindfulness practices within our lucid dreams. May the fusion of lucid dreaming and mindfulness bring us closer to a state of profound presence and self-discovery, unlocking the limitless potential within our dream world and waking lives. Get ready to delve into the depths of consciousness and embrace the transformative power that awaits us.

THE CONNECTION BETWEEN LUCID DREAMING AND MINDFULNESS

1. Understanding Mindfulness

Before we delve deeper into the connection between lucid dreaming and mindfulness, it is essential to gain a clear understanding of what mindfulness entails. Mindfulness is not a mere buzzword; it is a powerful practice that has been cultivated for centuries in various contemplative traditions. At its core, mindfulness is the practice of intentionally bringing one's attention to the present moment without judgment or attachment. It involves cultivating a state of heightened awareness and acceptance of one's thoughts, emotions, and sensations as they arise.

Mindfulness invites us to become observers of our own experiences, developing the capacity to witness our thoughts and emotions without getting entangled in them. It allows us to embrace the full spectrum of our human experience with curiosity and compassion, fostering a deep sense of self-acceptance and inner peace. By anchoring ourselves in the present moment, we can cultivate a deeper connection with ourselves, others, and the world around us.

2. Overlapping Qualities of Lucid Dreaming and Mindfulness

Lucid dreaming and mindfulness share several key qualities that make them compatible and complementary practices. Both involve the cultivation of awareness, the exploration of consciousness, and the development of a non-reactive mindset.

In lucid dreaming, we cultivate awareness by becoming conscious and self-aware within the dream state. We awaken to the fact that we are dreaming, and with this newfound awareness, we gain the ability to shape and navigate our dreams. Similarly, in mindfulness, we cultivate awareness by intentionally bringing our attention to the present moment. We become fully present with our thoughts, emotions, and sensations without getting caught up in the narratives they create. Both practices invite us to observe and engage with our experiences consciously.

Lucid dreaming and mindfulness also share a common ground in the exploration of consciousness. Lucid dreaming allows us to directly experience different states of consciousness and explore the boundless realms of our imagination. We can delve into the depths of our subconscious, encounter archetypal figures, and gain insights into our inner world. Mindfulness, too, involves an exploration of consciousness. By observing our thoughts and emotions without judgment, we begin to recognize the transient nature of our experiences and develop a deeper understanding of the ever-changing nature of our consciousness.

Furthermore, both lucid dreaming and mindfulness cultivate a non-reactive mindset. In lucid dreaming, we learn to respond to dream experiences with curiosity and openness rather than reacting impulsively. We can observe dream scenarios without getting entangled in the emotions they evoke. Similarly, mindfulness teaches us to observe our thoughts and emotions without judgment or attachment. We learn to witness our experiences without immediately reacting or being carried away by them. This non-reactive stance allows for greater clarity and equanimity in both dream and waking life.

3. Mindfulness as a Foundation for Lucid Dreaming

Practicing mindfulness during our waking lives serves as a solid foundation for lucid dreaming. By cultivating present-moment awareness and developing the ability to observe our thoughts and emotions without attachment, we enhance our self-reflective capacities. Mindfulness helps us become more attuned to the subtle cues and patterns within our waking experiences, which can then carry over into our dream lives.

Mindfulness allows us to cultivate a state of heightened self-awareness. By training our attention to remain focused on the present moment, we become more conscious of our thoughts, emotions, and physical sensations. This heightened self-awareness creates fertile ground for recognizing the dream state within our dreams. When we are more aware of our waking experiences, we are more likely to question our reality, leading to increased chances of becoming lucid within a dream.

Moreover, mindfulness enhances our ability to discern the subtle nuances of our inner landscape. By observing our thoughts and emotions without judgment, we develop a deeper understanding of our mental and emotional patterns. This awareness carries over into our dreams, where we can recognize recurring dream themes, emotions, and symbols. By noticing these patterns, we increase our chances of becoming lucid within a dream, as we can use them as triggers to question our reality.

The practice of mindfulness also cultivates a sense of openness and curiosity, which are essential qualities for lucid dreaming. When we approach our waking experiences with a non-judgmental attitude, we create space for curiosity and exploration. This mindset naturally extends into our dream lives, where we can approach dream scenarios with curiosity and openness. By embracing the unknown and being receptive to the possibilities within our dreams, we create fertile ground for lucidity to arise.

In addition to these aspects, mindfulness helps us develop a stable and focused mind, which is crucial for maintaining lucidity within a dream. By training our attention to remain anchored in the present moment, we enhance our ability to stay present and aware within the dream state. Mindfulness allows us to cultivate a clear and focused mind, reducing distractions and increasing our capacity to engage consciously with the dream environment.

In summary, mindfulness serves as a foundational practice for lucid dreaming by enhancing self-awareness, developing discernment of dream patterns, fostering curiosity and openness, and cultivating a stable and focused mind. As we cultivate mindfulness in our waking lives, we lay the groundwork for the integration of mindfulness within the realm of our dreams, facilitating the emergence of lucidity and deepening our exploration of consciousness.

TECHNIQUES FOR COMBINING LUCID DREAMING AND MINDFULNESS

1. Setting Mindful Intentions

One of the key aspects of combining lucid dreaming and mindfulness is setting mindful intentions before sleep. Intention setting is a powerful practice that allows us to direct our focus and energy towards a specific outcome. When it comes to lucid dreaming, setting intentions with a mindful approach can greatly enhance our chances of becoming lucid within a dream.

To set mindful intentions, find a quiet and comfortable space before bedtime. Begin by taking a few deep breaths, allowing yourself to relax and ground into the present moment. Reflect on your desire to cultivate mindfulness within your dreams and to become aware and conscious within the dream state. Clarify your intention to observe your thoughts, emotions, and sensations with non-judgmental awareness. Visualize yourself becoming lucid within a dream, engaging with the dream environment mindfully, and exploring with curiosity and openness.

As you set your intention, infuse it with a sense of presence and mindfulness. Connect with the feeling of being fully aware and engaged in the present moment. Allow yourself to feel the excitement and anticipation of experiencing lucidity in your dreams. By setting mindful intentions, you create a foundation for merging lucid dreaming and mindfulness, aligning your subconscious mind with your conscious desire for awareness and self-reflection.

2. Mindful Reality Testing

Reality testing is a widely used technique for inducing lucid dreams. It involves questioning the reality of your waking experience to determine whether you are dreaming or awake. By integrating mindfulness into reality testing, you can enhance your ability to recognize the dream state and increase your chances of becoming lucid.

When performing reality tests, approach them with a sense of curiosity and non-judgment. Instead of merely going through the motions, engage fully in the process. For example, when you perform a reality test such as checking the time, don't just glance at the clock and move on. Take a moment to truly observe the time, the position of the hands, and any other details. Notice the quality of your perception and the vividness of the scene. Cultivate a mindful awareness of the present moment and question the nature of your experience.

Incorporate mindfulness into other reality testing techniques as well. When you perform a nose pinch reality test, bring a sense of mindful awareness to the sensation of blocking your nose and attempting to breathe through it. Observe the sensations, thoughts, and emotions that arise during the test without judgment. By engaging in reality testing with mindfulness, you heighten your level of self-awareness and increase the likelihood of recognizing the dream state.

3. Mindful Engagement in Lucid Dreams

Once you achieve lucidity within a dream, the practice of mindfulness can greatly enhance your experience. Mindful engagement in lucid dreams involves approaching the dream environment with a non-reactive and curious mindset, observing your thoughts, emotions, and sensations without judgment, and fully immersing yourself in the present moment.

As you become aware that you are dreaming, take a moment to ground yourself in the dream environment.

Notice the details of your surroundings—the colors, textures, sounds, and smells. Engage your senses fully and bring a sense of mindful presence to the dream scene. By anchoring yourself in the present moment, you deepen your level of lucidity and enhance the vividness of the dream experience.

Throughout the lucid dream, practice mindful observation. Notice the thoughts and emotions that arise, allowing them to come and go without clinging to them. By cultivating a non-reactive stance, you can explore the dream environment with a sense of curiosity and openness. Observe the dream characters and objects, engage in conversations, and interact with the dream world mindfully. By bringing mindfulness to your actions and interactions within the dream, you deepen your level of engagement and self-awareness.

Additionally, use mindfulness techniques such as breath awareness or body scanning within the lucid dream. Bring your attention to your breath and notice its rhythm and sensations. Alternatively, scan your body from head to toe, observing any physical sensations or areas of tension. These practices help anchor you in the present moment, deepen your level of lucidity, and foster a sense of inner calm and presence within the dream state.

4. Dream Journaling with Mindfulness

Dream journaling is an essential practice for lucid dreamers, as it helps improve dream recall, identify dream patterns, and deepen self-reflection. When combining dream journaling with mindfulness, the process becomes even more potent and transformative.

Approach dream journaling with a mindful attitude. Before writing in your dream journal, take a moment to ground yourself in the present moment. Bring your attention to your breath and notice the sensations of the pen in your hand or the keyboard under your fingers. Allow yourself to be fully present with the act of journaling.

As you write, observe your thoughts and emotions as they arise without judgment or attachment. Notice the details of the dream as you recall them and describe them with clarity and precision. Engage all your senses as you vividly bring the dream to life through your writing. By practicing mindfulness during dream journaling, you deepen your connection with the dream experience and enhance your capacity for self-reflection and insight.

In addition to recording the events of the dream, take note of any emotional or sensory experiences you had during the dream. Reflect on the thoughts and feelings that arose within the dream and how they relate to your waking life. By bringing mindful awareness to your dream journaling practice, you develop a deeper understanding of the interplay between your dreams and your conscious experiences.

In conclusion, combining lucid dreaming with mindfulness offers a powerful synergy that enhances our ability to become aware and conscious within the dream state. By setting mindful intentions, engaging in reality testing with mindfulness, practicing mindful engagement within lucid dreams, and incorporating mindfulness into dream journaling, we deepen our connection to the present moment, expand our self-awareness, and unlock the transformative potential of lucid dreaming. Embrace the integration of mindfulness and lucid dreaming and embark on a journey of self-discovery and awakening within the realm of your dreams.

DEEPENING THE BENEFITS OF LUCID DREAMING THROUGH MINDFULNESS

1. Emotional Healing and Self-Discovery

Lucid dreaming, when combined with mindfulness, can be a powerful tool for emotional healing and self-discovery. Within the lucid dream state, we can explore and work through unresolved emotions, traumas, and patterns that may be impacting our waking lives.

With mindfulness as our guide, we approach emotional healing within the lucid dream with compassion and non-judgment. By observing our emotions and sensations without resistance or avoidance, we create a safe space for emotional exploration and release. We can consciously confront and process challenging emotions, allowing them to flow and transform within the dream.

During a lucid dream, when we encounter an emotionally charged situation or a symbol that represents a particular emotion, we can choose to engage with it mindfully. Instead of reacting impulsively, we can pause, observe our emotional response, and inquire into its origins and significance. By bringing mindful awareness to our emotional experiences within the dream, we gain valuable insights into our subconscious patterns and emotional landscapes.

Furthermore, mindfulness within the lucid dream allows us to engage in self-discovery and self-reflection. We can communicate with dream characters, who often represent aspects of our own psyche, and gain profound insights into our personality, desires, and fears. By mindfully engaging in conversations and interactions within the dream, we uncover hidden aspects of ourselves and deepen our self-understanding.

Through the integration of lucid dreaming and mindfulness, we create a bridge between the conscious and subconscious minds, opening up pathways for emotional healing and self-discovery. By approaching our dreams with mindfulness, we tap into the transformative potential of lucid dreaming and pave the way for personal growth and emotional well-being.

2. Enhancing Creativity and Problem-Solving

Lucid dreaming, when combined with mindfulness, can significantly enhance our creative abilities and problem-solving skills. In the lucid dream state, we have the freedom to explore our imagination, access unique perspectives, and tap into our creative potential.

By practicing mindfulness within the lucid dream, we bring a heightened sense of awareness and presence to the creative process. We can consciously shape and manipulate the dream environment by experimenting with different artistic mediums, exploring new ideas, and pushing the boundaries of our creativity. Mindfulness allows us to be fully engaged in the creative act, to observe our thoughts and inspirations as they arise, and to manifest them within the dream with clarity and intention.

Lucid dreaming also offers a safe space for creative exploration without the limitations and constraints of the waking world. We can engage in artistic endeavors, such as painting, writing, composing music, or choreographing dances, with an expanded sense of freedom and possibility. Within the dream, we can let go of self-judgment and expectations, allowing our creative expression to flow freely and authentically.

Moreover, mindfulness within the lucid dream enhances our problem-solving abilities. We can use lucid dreams to tackle challenges, find innovative solutions, and gain insights into complex issues. By engaging in mindful problem-solving within the dream state, we access the vast resources of our subconscious mind, tapping into our intuitive wisdom and expanding our perspectives. We can observe our thoughts, test different approaches, and gain clarity and understanding that can be applied to waking life situations.

The fusion of lucid dreaming and mindfulness offers fertile ground for creative exploration and problem-solving. By cultivating mindfulness within the lucid dream, we unlock our creative potential, expand our imagination, and tap into a wellspring of inspiration and innovation.

3. Spiritual Awakening and Transcendence

Combining lucid dreaming with mindfulness can be a profound catalyst for spiritual awakening and transcendence. Within the lucid dream state, we have the opportunity to explore the depths of our consciousness, connect with higher states of awareness, and experience a sense of unity and interconnectedness.

With mindfulness as our guiding principle, we approach the lucid dream as a spiritual journey, a gateway to the transcendent realms of consciousness. By cultivating mindful awareness within the dream, we deepen our capacity to observe the fluctuations of our mind, to disidentify from the ego, and to tap into the vastness of our true nature.

Within the lucid dream, we can engage in spiritual practices such as meditation, prayer, or contemplation. By bringing mindfulness to these practices, we enter into a state of deep presence and connection, transcending the limitations of the physical world and accessing higher dimensions of consciousness. We can experience profound states of bliss, oneness, and expanded awareness.

Lucid dreaming also offers an opportunity to connect with spiritual guides, archetypal figures, or symbolic representations of higher wisdom. By engaging in conversations with or receiving teachings from these entities, we gain profound insights into the nature of reality, our purpose, and the interconnectedness of all beings. Mindfulness allows us to approach these encounters with reverence, openness, and discernment.

Furthermore, lucid dreaming can serve as a bridge between our waking lives and spiritual experiences. By mindfully integrating our lucid dream experiences into our daily lives, we deepen our connection to the sacred and infuse our waking reality with spiritual meaning and purpose. We carry the insights and lessons from the lucid dream state into our waking consciousness, fostering a sense of interconnectedness, compassion, and transcendence.

The fusion of lucid dreaming and mindfulness opens a doorway to spiritual awakening and transcendence. By approaching the lucid dream state with mindful awareness, we delve into the depths of our consciousness, connect with higher realms of existence, and experience the profound union of the self and the universe.

In conclusion, by combining lucid dreaming and mindfulness, we unlock the full potential of both practices. Mindfulness serves as a guiding principle that deepens our self-awareness, enhances our engagement within lucid dreams, and amplifies the transformative effects of the lucid dream state. Through mindfulness, we can harness the power of lucid dreaming for emotional healing, self-discovery, enhanced creativity, problem-solving, spiritual awakening, and transcendence. Embrace the integration of lucid dreaming and mindfulness and embark on a journey of self-exploration, growth, and awakening within the realm of your dreams.

CONCLUSION

Throughout this chapter, we have explored the profound potential that arises from the integration of lucid dreaming and mindfulness. By combining these practices, we unlock a pathway to personal transformation, self-discovery, enhanced creativity, emotional healing, problem-solving, and spiritual awakening. The synergy between lucid dreaming and mindfulness creates fertile ground for exploration, growth, and profound experiences within the realm of dreams.

Lucid dreaming, the ability to become aware and conscious within the dream state, offers a gateway to the depths of our subconscious mind. It allows us to access the hidden recesses of our psyche, confront unresolved emotions, and gain insights into our patterns, desires, and fears. Lucidity within dreams empowers us to shape and influence the dream environment, opening up possibilities for creativity, problem-solving, and self-expression.

Mindfulness, on the other hand, is a practice of cultivating present-moment awareness, non-judgmental observation, and acceptance. It deepens our connection to the present moment and expands our self-awareness. By applying mindfulness within the realm of lucid dreaming, we bring a heightened sense of consciousness, intentionality, and clarity to our dream experiences.

By setting mindful intentions before sleep, engaging in reality testing with mindfulness, practicing mindful engagement within lucid dreams, and incorporating mindfulness into dream journaling, we create a powerful foundation for merging lucid dreaming and mindfulness. These techniques allow us to cultivate self-awareness, explore the depths of our consciousness, and tap into the transformative potential of the dream state.

The fusion of lucid dreaming and mindfulness offers numerous benefits and opportunities for personal growth. When we approach our dreams with mindfulness, we deepen our connection to the present moment, expand our awareness, and develop a more profound relationship with ourselves. Through lucid dreaming, we can explore our creativity, engage in problem-solving, and tap into the wellspring of inspiration and innovation.

Moreover, lucid dreaming with mindfulness can be a catalyst for emotional healing and self-discovery. Within the dream state, we can consciously confront and process unresolved emotions, traumas, and patterns. By practicing mindfulness within the lucid dream, we create a safe space for emotional exploration, release, and integration. We gain valuable insights into our subconscious landscape, uncover hidden aspects of ourselves, and deepen our self-understanding.

The combination of lucid dreaming and mindfulness also holds immense potential for spiritual awakening and transcendence. By cultivating mindful awareness within the lucid dream, we access higher states of consciousness, experience profound interconnectedness, and engage in spiritual practices within the dream realm. Lucid dreaming becomes a portal to the sacred, a means to connect with spiritual guides, receive teachings, and transcend the limitations of the physical world.

As we embrace the integration of lucid dreaming and mindfulness, we embark on a transformative journey of self-exploration, growth, and awakening. It is an invitation to dive deep into the ocean of our consciousness to unlock the wisdom and potential that lie within. Lucid dreaming with mindfulness becomes a sacred practice, a gateway to profound experiences and insights that ripple into our waking lives.

In closing, I invite you to embark on your own lucid dreaming and mindfulness journey. Embrace the techniques, principles, and practices shared within this chapter as tools for self-discovery, growth, and personal transformation. Cultivate present-moment awareness, set mindful intentions, engage in reality testing, practice mindful engagement within your lucid dreams, and journal your experiences with mindfulness. Explore the depths of your consciousness, unleash your creativity, heal unresolved emotions, solve problems, and open yourself to the mysteries and wonders of the dream realm.

Remember, lucid dreaming and mindfulness are not just practices confined to the realm of dreams but gifts that extend into your waking life. As you integrate the wisdom and insights gained from lucid dreaming into your everyday experiences, you deepen your connection to yourself, others, and the world around you. Embrace the power of lucid dreaming with mindfulness and embark on a transformative journey of self-discovery, personal growth, and spiritual awakening.

Conclusion

In this transformative journey through the realm of lucid dreaming, we have delved deep into the mysteries of the sleeping mind and explored the incredible power that lies within our dreams. Throughout this book, we have uncovered the definition and history of lucid dreaming, examined the science behind it, and learned various techniques for inducing and controlling lucid dreams. We have also explored the profound impact that lucid dreaming can have on our creative expression, healing and self-discovery, and the integration of mindfulness into our dream states.

As we reach the conclusion of this book, it is essential to reflect on the incredible possibilities that lucid dreaming offers us. Lucid dreaming is not merely a whimsical escape into a fantastical world; it is a gateway to self-realization, personal growth, and profound insights into the nature of reality. By harnessing the power of lucid dreams, we can unlock the hidden potentials of our minds and transform our lives in ways we never thought possible.

Throughout our exploration, we have discovered that lucid dreaming holds the potential to enhance our creativity. The lucid dream state allows us to break free from the limitations of the waking world and explore the depths of our imagination. Within our dreams, we can paint vivid landscapes, compose breathtaking music, and write captivating stories. Lucid dreaming becomes a playground for artists, writers, musicians, and creatives of all kinds, providing a limitless canvas for the manifestation of our innermost desires and inspirations. By tapping into this wellspring of creativity, we can not only enhance our artistic pursuits but also uncover innovative solutions to real-world challenges.

In addition to fostering creativity, lucid dreaming offers a powerful tool for healing and self-discovery. Within the safe confines of the dream world, we can confront and heal emotional traumas, explore the depths of our subconscious, and gain valuable insights into our fears, desires, and aspirations. Lucid dreams provide a platform for self-reflection and self-improvement, enabling us to uncover the patterns and belief systems that shape our lives. By working with our dreams, we can identify areas for personal growth, overcome obstacles, and cultivate a deeper sense of self-awareness and self-compassion. Lucid dreaming becomes a transformative practice that allows us to integrate our past, present, and future selves, leading to greater wholeness and fulfillment.

Mindfulness, the art of being fully present in the present moment, finds a natural synergy with lucid dreaming. By bringing the principles of mindfulness into our dreams, we can deepen our lucidity, enhance our sensory experiences, and cultivate a profound sense of awe and appreciation for the dream world. Lucid dreaming becomes a spiritual practice, a way to explore the interconnectedness of all things and dissolve the boundaries between the dream and waking states. Through the marriage of lucid dreaming and mindfulness, we can develop a heightened sense of consciousness and live more consciously in our waking lives.

As we conclude this book, let us not forget the practical techniques that serve as gateways to lucid dreaming. Reality testing, a simple yet powerful tool, allows us to question our reality and establish a habit of critical awareness that carries over into our dreams. Wake-Initiated Lucid Dreaming (WILD) and Mnemonic-Induced Lucid Dreaming (MILD) provide structured approaches to induce lucidity, each with its own unique benefits and challenges. Exploring other techniques such as Wake-Back-to-Bed (WBTB) and Finger Induced Lucid Dreaming (FILD) expands our repertoire and empowers us to find the method that resonates most with our individual needs and preferences. By combining these techniques with patience, perseverance, and a genuine curiosity for the dream world, we can open the doors to lucid dreaming and embark on an extraordinary adventure.

However, embarking on this journey is not without its challenges. Lucid dreaming requires dedication, practice, and a willingness to explore the depths of our own consciousness. It is essential to approach lucid dreaming with respect, responsibility, and ethical considerations. As we delve into the realm of dreams, we must maintain a balance between exploration and self-care, ensuring that our lucid dreaming practice supports our overall well-being. It is also crucial to remember that lucid dreaming is a highly individual experience, and each dreamer's journey will be unique. Comparisons and expectations can hinder our progress, so it is vital to embrace our own path and honor our personal growth.

As we conclude this book, I invite you to take a moment to reflect on the knowledge and insights you have gained. You hold within you the keys to unlocking the boundless potential of lucid dreaming. It is now up to you to take action, to step into the realm of dreams and claim the power that awaits you there. Begin by incorporating reality testing into your daily life, questioning the nature of your reality and fostering self-awareness. Experiment with different techniques for inducing and controlling lucid dreams, discovering which methods resonate most with you. Embrace the creative, healing, and self-discovery potential of lucid dreaming, allowing your dreams to become a canvas for your aspirations and a source of deep personal transformation. And finally, integrate mindfulness into your lucid dreams, merging the waking and dream states to deepen your consciousness and appreciation for the present moment.

Remember, this book is not the end of your journey but the beginning. The real magic lies in your firsthand experiences, in the dreams that unfold before you, and the insights you gain along the way. Embrace the adventure, relish the wonder, and be open to the limitless possibilities that lucid dreaming offers. Your dreams are waiting to be explored, and your potential is waiting to be realized. It is time to awaken to the power of lucid dreaming and embark on a lifelong journey of self-discovery, creativity, and transformation.

So, my fellow dreamers, go forth with courage, curiosity, and a sense of wonder. Embrace the hidden realms of your dreams and unlock the vast potentials that lie within. As you navigate the ever-shifting landscapes of your dreamscapes, remember that you hold the power to shape your dreams and, ultimately, your waking life. Lucid dreaming is not just a dream; it is a reality waiting to be explored. It is a gateway to the extraordinary, a source of limitless inspiration, and a profound mirror reflecting the depths of your being.

Now, close this book and open your eyes to the boundless possibilities that await you in the world of lucid dreaming. Your journey has just begun.

Sweet dreams and awakenings!

Bibliography

Books:

- LaBerge, S., & Rheingold, H. (1991). Exploring the World of Lucid Dreaming. Ballantine Books.
- Waggoner, R., & McCready, C. (2009). Lucid Dreaming: Gateway to the Inner Self. Moment Point Press.
- Green, C. E. (1990). Lucid Dreams. Citadel Press.
- Yuschak, T. (2006). Advanced Lucid Dreaming: The Power of Supplements. Lulu.com.
- Garfield, P. (1974). Creative Dreaming. Simon & Schuster.
- Tart, C. T. (1987). Altered States of Consciousness: A Book of Readings. Wiley.
- Fariba Bogzaran, Daniel Deslauriers, & Stanley Krippner. (2017). Extraordinary

Dreams and How to Work with Them. State University of New York Press.

Scientific Papers and Research Articles:

- LaBerge, S. (1985). Lucid Dreaming: The Power of Being Awake and Aware in Your Dreams. In Sleep and Cognition (pp. 109-126). American Psychological Association.
- Erlacher, D., & Schredl, M. (2008). Reality testing and physiological parameter changes in lucid dreams. Applied Psychophysiology and Biofeedback, 33(1), 41-56.
- Voss, U., Holzmann, R., Tuin, I., & Hobson, A. (2009). Lucid dreaming: a state of consciousness with features of both waking and non-lucid dreaming. Sleep, 32(9), 1191-1200.
- Stumbrys, T., Erlacher, D., & Schädlich, M. (2012). Induction of lucid dreams: A systematic review of evidence. Consciousness and Cognition, 21(3), 1456-1475.

Websites and Online Resources:

- Lucidity Institute. (n.d.). Retrieved from https://www.lucidity.com/

- International Association for the Study of Dreams (IASD). (n.d.). Retrieved from https://www.asdreams.org/
- World of Lucid Dreaming. (n.d.). Retrieved from https://www.world-of-lucid-dreaming.com/
- Exploring Your Mind. (n.d.). Retrieved from https://exploringyourmind.com/

THANK YOU!

I wanted to thank you for taking the time to purchase my book. I hope you enjoyed it and found it informative.

If you enjoyed the book and are looking for more, you can sign up for my newsletter. I'll be sending out updates about new books, events, and other exciting news!

Signing up is effortless – all you need to do is scan the QR code below and enter your details.

Thanks again for your support and I look forward to seeing you around!

Best wishes,
Casey Williams

www.ingramcontent.com/pod-product-compliance
Lightning Source LLC
Chambersburg PA
CBHW070118100426
42744CB00010B/1856